The NAUTI-BENDER 900
Question & Answer

SKIPPER'S CHALLENGE

SEAMANSHIP & SMALL BOAT HANDLING

Dale R. Lydigsen

PENCHANT PUBLISHING
Post Office Box 109
Jackson, New Hampshire 03846

SKIPPER'S CHALLENGE

Published By: Penchant Publishing

Author: Dale R. Lydigsen, Jr.

First Edition: 1998

ISBN: 0-9643108-3-X

Library of Congress Catalog Card Number: 98-91659

Printed: In Hong Kong

Purchase Information: For sales/ordering inquiries, special pric-
ing, or information on where to purchase Penchant Publishing's
books and calendars contact our sales department at 800-235-7221
or fax 603-383-8108.

PHONE 603-383-4505   Post Office Box 109   FAX 603-383-8108
Jackson, New Hampshire 03846

PUBLISHER'S ACKNOWLEDGEMENTS

We're proud of this book and plan to continue publishing it for many years to come. To help maintain the highest standards of quality and accuracy... we would welcome any comments you may have (good and bad). Please send to our Editorial Department (Penchant Publishing, P.O. Box 109, Jackson, NH 03846).

Also, we would like to express our appreciation and sincere thanks to the many individuals that have contributed to this book's publication:

Technical Consultants: Captains: Vince Tibbetts, Dick Winchell, Jon Whales, Doug Moore, Don DaCosta, and Al Stephens.

Editors: Peggy Schleicher, Bill Marvel, Donna Stuart, Elizabeth Dempsey, and Josh Knox.

Art Design: Maureen Rupp, Gayle Lemeri, Jodie Neal, Bill Nicholson, Stephen Mudgett, and Mark Nelson.

Special Thanks To: Debbie Cloutier, Mike Sipsey, Paula Tibbetts and Ray Burke.

Cover Photo Credits: Photo by Carlo Borlenghi/Stock Newport.

TABLE OF CONTENTS

TABLE OF CONTENTS

Author's Introduction

"Seamanship" is having a good sense of the sea, boats and how they react together in an ever-changing environment.

Every marina has their share of "Mr. Magoos", who "require assistance" on a constant basis. You name it and the Mr. Magoos have it – mechanical, electrical, electronic, and especially engine/fuel problems. Once underway, their antics spawn a whole new host of nicknames... like "crash" or "fend-off" and many well known rocks, ledges, and shoal areas are affectionately renamed after them.

On the other hand, at every marina there are also skippers who seemingly handle every situation effortlessly with the greatest of ease. Obviously, the difference between the Mr. Magoos and the skippers is good seamanship. It is typically a lack or lapse of this sense that gets boaters into trouble while on-the-water.

One is not born with good seamanship, it is acquired through education and experience. A skipper's challenge is two-fold: the subject is complex/comprehensive and the vast majority of recreational boaters are on-the-water only on a part-time or seasonal basis... skills get rusty.

With the above in mind, our **Skipper's Challenge** was developed to help boaters shortcut the school of "hard rocks", learn new things, measure and most importantly **maintain** their skills. This book was written especially for recreational boaters and emphasizes the practical day-to-day seamanship knowledge required to safely enjoy their favorite pastime.

On a final note, many individuals have conscientiously contributed to this book; however, if you have any suggestions for improvement (or locate any of our "Mr. Magoos") please let us know. We enjoy hearing what our readers have to say.

Dale R. Lydigsen

ABOUT THIS BOOK

Format: the game-like, question & answer format is offered as a fun alternative to the somewhat "dry" reading typical of most nautical reference manuals.

Subject Matter: "Nauti-Bender" questions range from simple to complex and are organized by subject in a random fashion like the skills needed while on-the-water. However, the handy thumb index (back cover) and the associated tabs (on each page) can be utilized to re-visit the more troublesome subjects.

Answers: Given the nature of the book, it was not intended nor does the format lend itself to lengthy explanation... therefore, it is suggested that a good reference manual be referred to if required. The Nauti-Bender answers were purposely placed on the next facing page to discourage "shortcuts over shoal waters".

Where to Start: Beginners or novices should probably review the "language" category initially. Others can go from the beginning to the end or category by category... their choice.

Review: To stay as seaworthy as your boat... we recommend that the "Challenge" be reviewed on a regular basis.

Good Luck!!

The term "_____ _____" originated on early naval vessels· where the lavatory facilities were typically located topside at the foremost part of the ship.

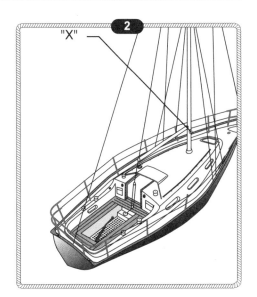

Sail Language: "**X**", shown above, would be referred to as the _____ _____ _____.

Answers

*The answers to the Nauti-Benders in this book are given on the **next facing page**.*

For example, the answers for the above are given on page 4.

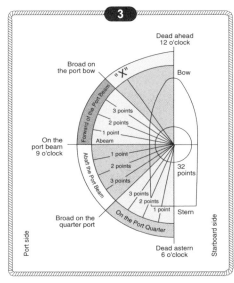

Language Under Way: an object bearing at point "**X**" (shown above) would be referred to as a "_____ _____ on the port bow".

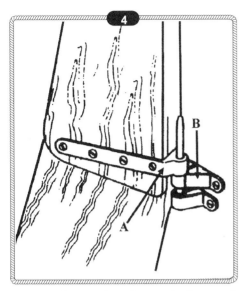

A rudder fitting referred to as the "_____" (**A** shown above) is the eye socket into which the "_____" (**B** shown above) is slipped to form a hinge about which the rudder pivots.

A triangular, rectangular, or swallowtailed flag usually associated with a yacht club membership is called a "_____".

Horizontal Anchor Windlass

Windlass Nomenclature: "**A**" shown above is referred to as the "_____ _____" which disengages the chain links and typically feeds the chain into the chain locker.

NAUTI-BENDER
Answers

*The answers to the Nauti-Benders in this book are given on the **next facing page**.*

For example, the answers for the above are given on page 5.

BOAT HANDLING

Caught in a squall, which sail would normally come down first?

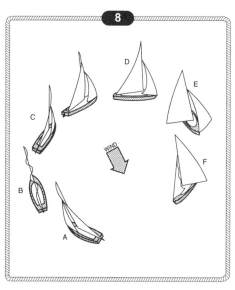

Which vessel is in the process of "coming about"?

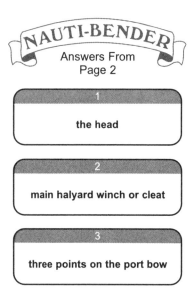

NAUTI-BENDER

Answers From
Page 2

1

the head

2

main halyard winch or cleat

3

three points on the port bow

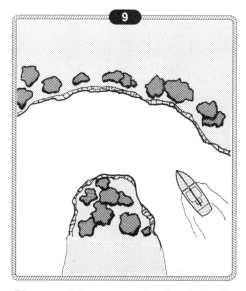

River cruising general rule-of-thumb: running downstream, stay in the _____ of the channel; when heading upstream, stay as close to the _____ bank as possible.

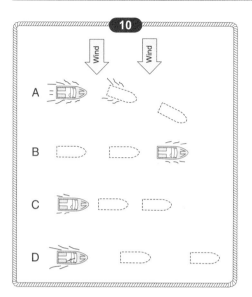

The effect of wind on exposed areas of a vessel is **most** noticeable when: (A) **turning**, (B) **backing**, (C) **going slow ahead**, or (D) **going full ahead**?

After being underway for a couple hours, your engine is running very hot. Most likely: (A) **the raw-water intake is clogged**, (B) **the thermostat is stuck shut**, or (C) **the raw-water impeller has failed**?

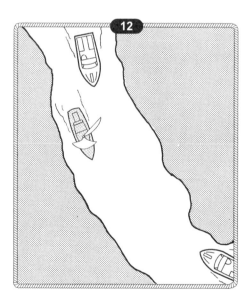

A vessel proceeding up a shallow, narrow channel may experience "bank suction". This phenomenon will force the stern or bow **away** or **toward** the nearest bank.

NAUTI-BENDER
Answers From
Page 3

4
A: gudgeon
B: pintle

5
burgee

6
chain stripper

13

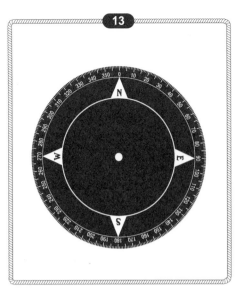

The four principal compass points: North, South, East, and West are commonly referred to as "_____ _____".

14

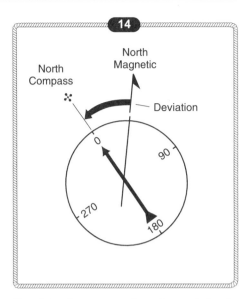

If cruising in an area where the variation is West, the compass course will be _____ than the true course.

NAUTI-BENDER
Answers From Page 4

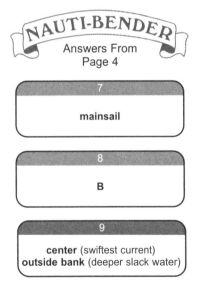

7

mainsail

8

B

9

center (swiftest current)
outside bank (deeper slack water)

15

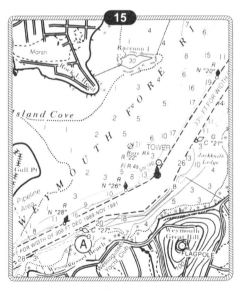

Nautical charts utilize _____ lettering to label all information about objects that are **not** affected by tide or current.

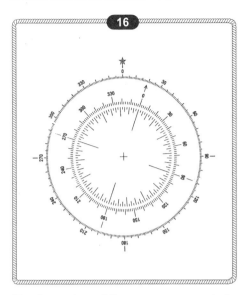

The inner ring of the compass rose indicates _____ bearings.

There are how many "points" in a mariner's circle?

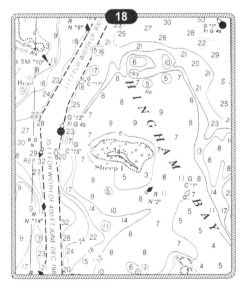

Nautical chart lettering: slanted or italic lettering is used to label all information about objects that are affected by _____ _____ or _____.

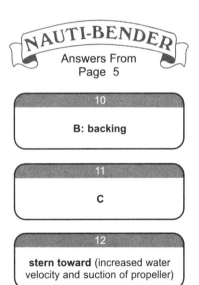

NAUTI-BENDER
Answers From
Page 5

10
B: backing

11
C

12
stern toward (increased water velocity and suction of propeller)

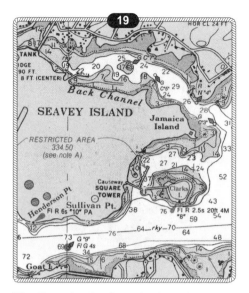

The first rule of safe anchoring: **always** or **never** anchor to the **leeward** or **windward** of the shore.

Given a "slack" current, boats at anchor or moored will ride **into** or **with** the wind?

NAUTI-BENDER

Answers From
Page 6

13
Cardinal Points

14
greater

15
straight

What is the rule-of-thumb when anchoring as to the ratio of **rode** to **depth-of-water**?

Adding a length of chain between the anchor rode and the anchor increases holding power and reduces bottom chafe. In general, the chain should be the boat's length plus _____ feet.

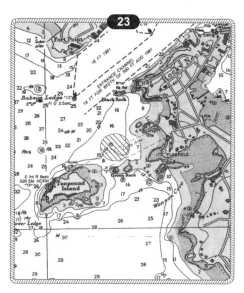

The shaded area off Ten-Pound Island would offer an excellent anchorage when the prevailing wind is **Northeast** or **Southwest**.

Before anchoring, what is the **most** important consideration: (A) **holding ground**; (B) **the number, type, and position of boats present and anticipated**; (C) **anticipated winds/weather**; or (D) **water depth, current direction, tidal range**?

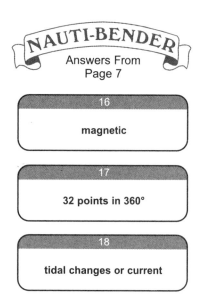

NAUTI-BENDER
Answers From
Page 7

16
magnetic

17
32 points in 360°

18
tidal changes or current

"Can" buoys are **even** or **odd** numbered?

Which buoys are typically lettered vs. numbered: **green can buoys**, **red nun buoys**, **preferred channel bouys**, and/or **cardinal buoys**?

NAUTI-BENDER
Answers From
Page 8

19
always leeward
never windward

20
into

21
5 to 7 times depth

Cruising in open water, the mate sights a float with a small flag in the distance, indicating a: **fishnet**, **race marker**, **sunken vessel**, **diver**, or **all of the above**?

Day markers, normally square or triangular shaped, are typically used in _____ _____ to mark channels.

A cylindrical buoy, tapering at the top and typically red in color, is called a "_____" buoy.

A white buoy (orange stripes) as shown above indicates?

NAUTI-BENDER
Answers From Page 9

22
five

23
Southwest

24
anticipated winds/weather

A good captain will always make sure that the crew knows what their duties are well before _____ or _____ a berth.

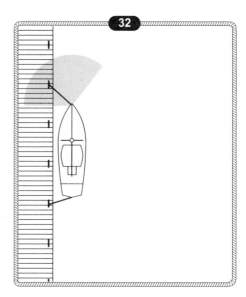

When departing (as shown above), with wind forward of the beam, the skipper should leave **bow** or **stern** first.

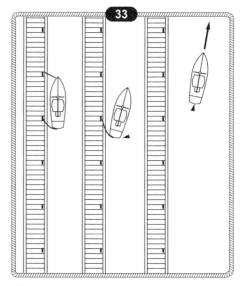

The above unberthing procedure would be proper with wind and tide coming from **ahead** or **astern**?

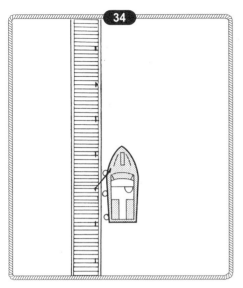

When docking port side-to and being set off by a strong wind you're able to get a spring line from your inside forward cleat to the dock, the vessel will come alongside easily by putting your port engine _____ and your starboard engine _____.

When docking, after considering wind/tide etc., planning the maneuver and instructing the crew, the well-prepared skipper will also have a pre-selected _____ route should it be needed.

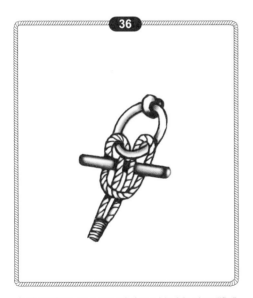

A short bar or a wood dowel is ideal to "fix" an eye to a ring and **can** or **cannot** be easily released under load.

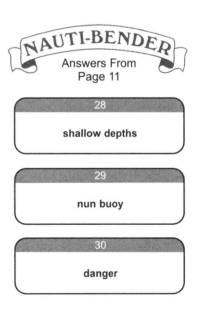

NAUTI-BENDER
Answers From
Page 11

28
shallow depths

29
nun buoy

30
danger

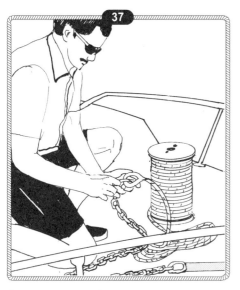

Some docks don't have cleats and utilize posts for tying up boats. In this situation two _____ _____ can be easily "looped" over the top of the post to secure the boat.

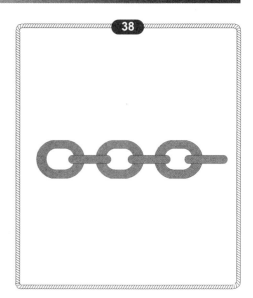

Chain size is referred to by the _____ of any part of the individual links, measured in increments of inches (e.g. 3/16", 1/4", 5/16" etc.).

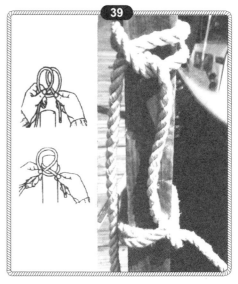

Ropes are called "_____" when they are rigged for a specific purpose onboard, except when rigged to the anchor; if so, the rope is called an anchor "_____".

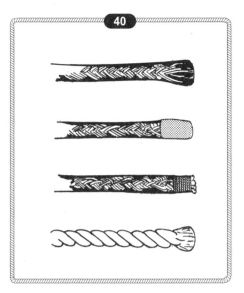

Lines are "_____" on the ends to prevent fraying or unraveling.

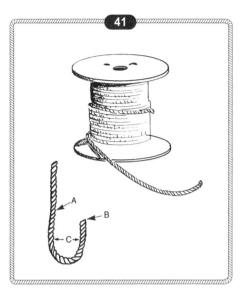

Line Nomenclature: identify "**A**", "**B**", and "**C**" shown above. A "hank" of line is how long?

When moored or anchored, a vessel's mooring lines should be protected with some type of "_____ _____".

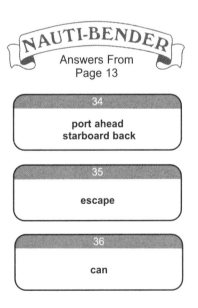

NAUTI-BENDER
Answers From
Page 13

34
port ahead
starboard back

35
escape

36
can

First rule of boating: "one hand for
_____ and one for the _____ ".

The water-ski hand-signal shown above
indicates: _____ _____ _____ _____.

NAUTI-BENDER

Answers From
Page 14

37

clove hitches

38

diameter

39

lines
rode

Most minor petroleum spills are caused by
_____ _____.

_____ _____ and sails flapping in the breeze are the major enemies of synthetic sails.

The clock shown above is indicating 12 p.m. _____ hours and should be ringing _____ bells.

Are your trailer lights burning out a lot? Try _____ lights before backing down ramp (cold water and hot lights don't mix).

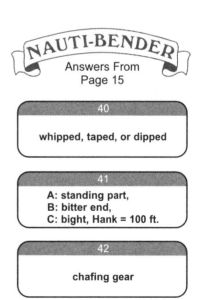

NAUTI-BENDER
Answers From
Page 15

40
whipped, taped, or dipped

41
A: standing part, **B: bitter end,** **C: bight, Hank = 100 ft.**

42
chafing gear

Safe speed, is the speed at which you can take proper corrective action to avoid _____.

More control can be achieved when running downwind in heavy weather by trailing long "_____" in a "_____".

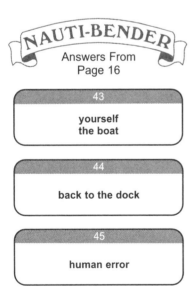

NAUTI-BENDER
Answers From
Page 16

43

yourself
the boat

44

back to the dock

45

human error

Approaching a closed bridge at night (up current) you hold back at a respectful distance. Then you observe a _____ light moving up and down indicating that you should _____.

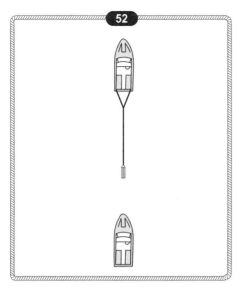

When cruising with another vessel, the above technique would be quite useful in _____ _____.

When going aground, the proper procedure is to gun the engine(s) astern immediately: **true** or **false**?

"_____ _____" spinnakers combine the radial, horizontal, and star-cut designs, producing an excellent all-purpose sail.

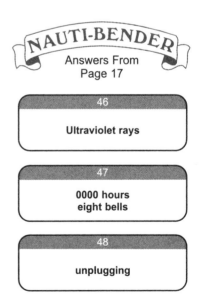

NAUTI-BENDER
Answers From Page 17

46

Ultraviolet rays

47

**0000 hours
eight bells**

48

unplugging

Smoke from exhaust (gasoline engine): _____ smoke is the normal color for two-stroke engine and indicates internal wear in a four-stroke engine.

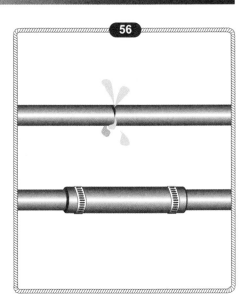

Having trouble slipping on a tight hose or getting hose-type chafing gear slipped over a line? The difficulty may be eliminated by lubricating the items with _____ _____ _____.

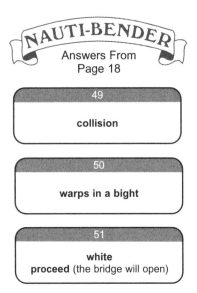

NAUTI-BENDER
Answers From Page 18

49
collision

50
warps in a bight

51
white **proceed** (the bridge will open)

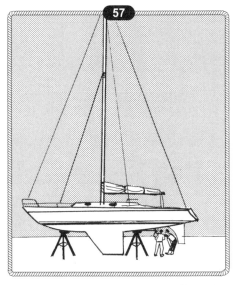

Boat winterizing should include filling the inboard fuel tank(s) to **1/4**, **1/2**, or **F** and adding a stabilizer?

Rather than discharging toxic cleaners overboard, unclog sink drains or heads by flushing _____ _____ followed by boiling water through the lines.

Smoke from exhaust (diesel engine): a faulty injector (insufficient fuel) or poor compression (fuel not igniting) will produce _____ smoke.

Spraying flags, bungees, ensigns, etc. with Scotch Guard™ will prolong their lives (especially in salt-water areas) up to _____ times normal.

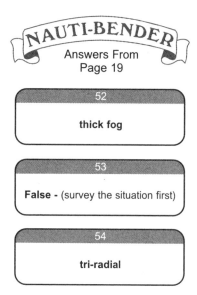

NAUTI-BENDER
Answers From Page 19

52

thick fog

53

False - (survey the situation first)

54

tri-radial

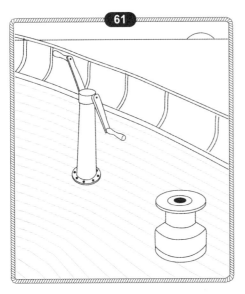

A powerful sheet winch used on sophisticated racing yachts is referred to as a " _____ _____ ".

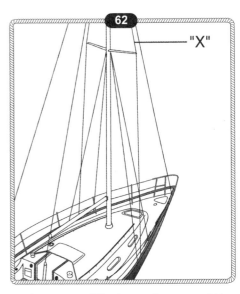

"X"

Sail language "**X**", shown above, would be referred to as the _____ _____.

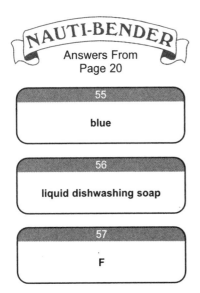

NAUTI-BENDER
Answers From
Page 20

55
blue

56
liquid dishwashing soap

57
F

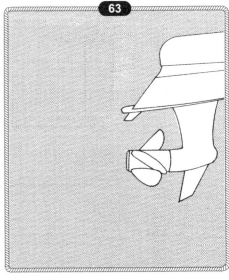

The inverted fin at the lowest point of an outboard or I/O is referred to as the " _____ ".

64

Anchor Nomenclature: "**X**" shown above would be referred to as the "_____".

65

The inward curving of the topsides above the waterline is referrred to as "_____".

66

The above vessel is referred to as a "_____".

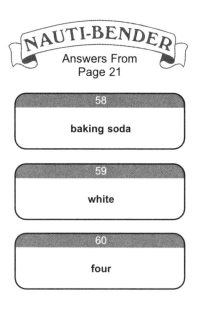

NAUTI-BENDER
Answers From
Page 21

58

baking soda

59

white

60

four

A powerboat not making way in restricted visibility should sound _____ prolonged blast(s) every two minutes.

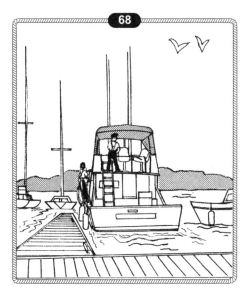

A power-driven vessel when leaving a dock or a berth should sound _____ prolonged blast(s).

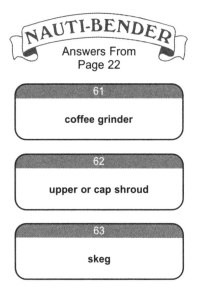

NAUTI-BENDER
Answers From Page 22

61

coffee grinder

62

upper or cap shroud

63

skeg

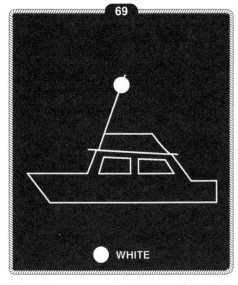

WHITE

The above vessel's light configuration would indicate she is _____.

You are approaching a drawbridge that will open any time upon request. What signal should be sounded to request the bridge be opened?

A sailing vessel in fog should sound a _____ followed by _____ _____ blasts every two minutes.

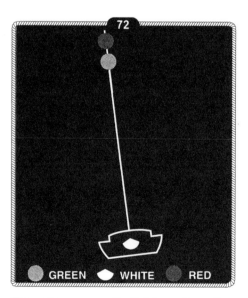

GREEN ◆ WHITE ● RED

The above vessel's light configuration would indicate she is a _____.

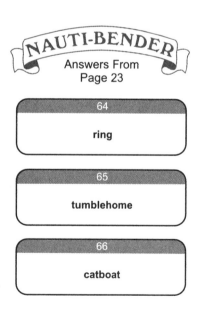

When docking, which line should usually be secured first (99% of the time)?

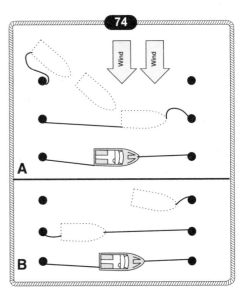

Berthing in a restricted space using fore-and-aft mooring buoys or between piles sometimes can be difficult. Which approach, "**A**" or "**B**" (shown above) would be easier in strong cross-wind conditions?

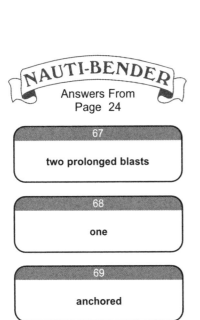

NAUTI-BENDER
Answers From
Page 24

67
two prolonged blasts

68
one

69
anchored

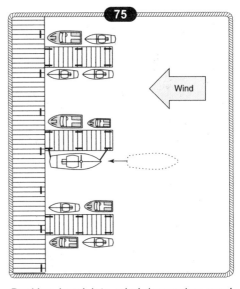

Docking head into wind (assuming good reverse control): motor in, use forward burst to stop the boat's momentum, and secure the _____ line first.

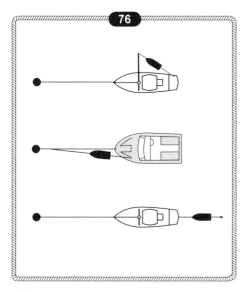

When moored or anchored, a bumping dinghy can be damaging to both the vessel and the crew's sleep. Avoid the bumping by rigging a _____ _____ to the mooring or boom or by trailing a _____ off the dinghy's stern.

Remember, if everyone tries to fend off on the same side, the boat may heel and tangle her "_____".

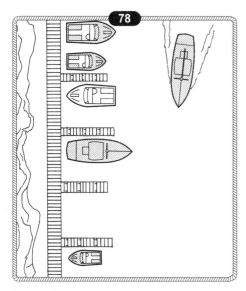

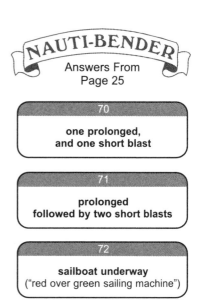

NAUTI-BENDER
Answers From Page 25

70

one prolonged,
and one short blast

71

prolonged
followed by two short blasts

72

sailboat underway
("red over green sailing machine")

Generally, you have more steering control when docking **bow** or **stern** in?

79

Lighthouses flashing alternating lights of different colors can have two ranges of visibility – one for white and another, _____ percent shorter, for red or green.

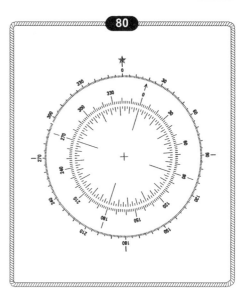

80

The outer ring of the compass rose indicates "_____" bearings.

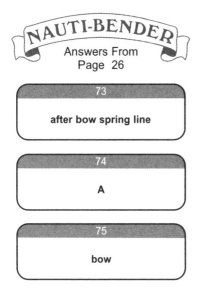

NAUTI-BENDER
Answers From
Page 26

73

after bow spring line

74

A

75

bow

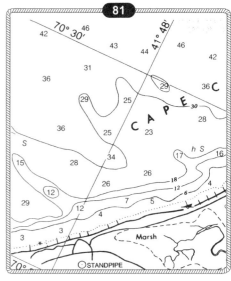

81

Horizontal or **vertical** lines on nautical charts are called meridians of longitude and are angular measurements of distance _____ or _____ of the prime meridian located at _____ _____.

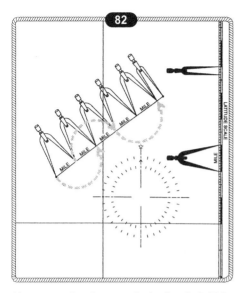

How many feet in a nautical mile: **A**. 5,280, **B**. 6,076, **C**. 6,650, or **D**. 5,980?

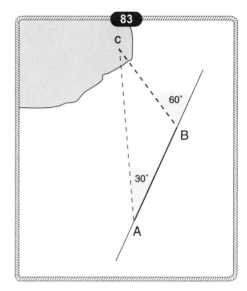

The above illustrates a simple method for calculating distance (**A** to **B** = **B** to **C**) using "relative" bearings called: "_____ _____ _____ _____ _____ _____".

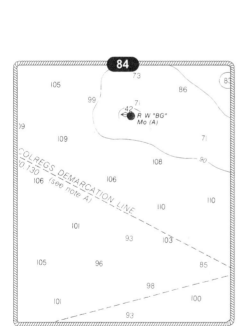

Some **notes** and _____ **navigational aids** are highlighted on nautical charts in a magenta-colored ink because the color is easily read under a _____ light.

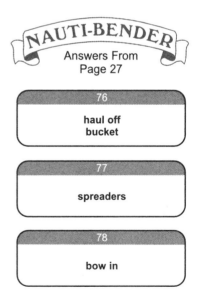

NAUTI-BENDER
Answers From
Page 27

76
haul off
bucket

77
spreaders

78
bow in

Many collisions occur on the edge of fog; therefore the rule: "sound signals must be sounded _____ or _____ an area of restricted visibility".

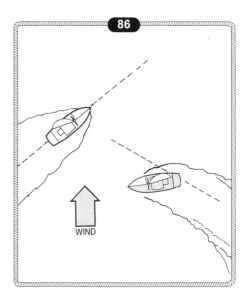

The boat with the right-of-way in a head-on crossing situation is referred to as the _____-_____ vessel.

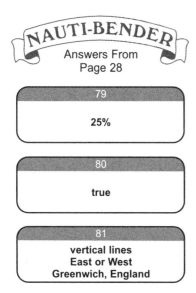

NAUTI-BENDER

Answers From
Page 28

79
25%

80
true

81
vertical lines **East or West** **Greenwich, England**

The operator of a self-propelled vessel 39' 4-1/2" or more in length (operating on inland waters) is required by law to carry on board a copy of the Inland Navigation Rules – **true** or **false**.

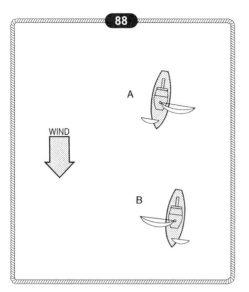

Which boat has the right-of-way?

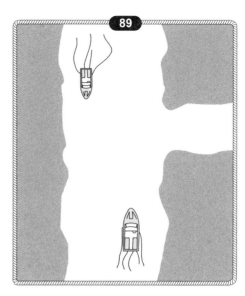

In the above meeting situation (no current or tide), assuming both vessels are going to turn into the smaller channel at approximately the same time, who has the right of way?

EPIRBs have a readiness test switch to check for proper operation. Tests should be conducted for _____ second(s) during the first _____ minutes of the hour to avoid false alarms.

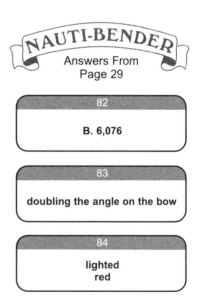

NAUTI-BENDER
Answers From
Page 29

82

B. 6,076

83

doubling the angle on the bow

84

**lighted
red**

91

When retrieving the anchor, what is the term used to indicate the anchor has cleared the bottom?

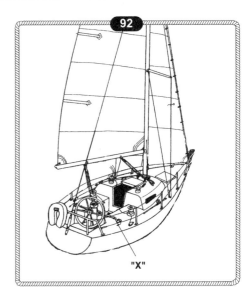

92

"X"

Sail Language: "**X**" shown above would be referred to as the "_____" and is a sail control system that moves the mainsheet from side-to-side on the boat.

NAUTI-BENDER
Answers From
Page 30

85

in or near

86

stand-on

87

true

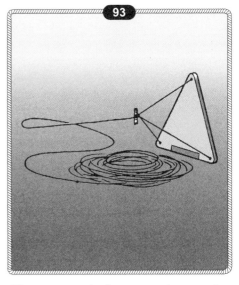

93

"The _____ log", a speed-measuring device, is dropped off the stern; the line is knotted every 23.3 feet, and the number of "**knots**" that run out in 15 seconds equals the vessel's speed.

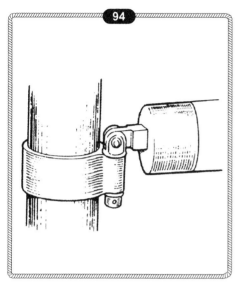

94

The metal fitting on the inboard end of a boom which allows movement in all directions is referred to as the: (A) **lizard**, (B) **spider band**, (C) **boom swiveler**, or (D) **gooseneck**.

95

To "_____" a line is to lead it through an opening (eye, block, thimble, etc.).

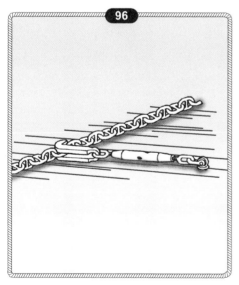

96

"_____ _____": a deck fitting used on larger vessels to temporarily prevent the anchor chain from running out, thereby taking the strain off the windlass.

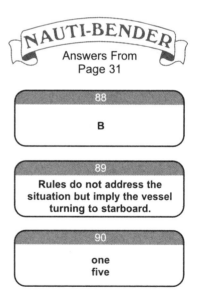

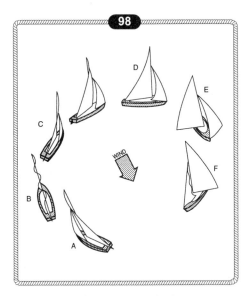

Salvage Claims: clearly establish the helper's terms before accepting a tow. Also, if possible use **your** or the **would be rescuer's** tow line indicating a "voluntary acceptance of aid".

To maintain forward speed when maneuvering from close-reach to a broad-reach, you should: **ease** or **haul** in the sheets and shift weight **inboard** or **outboard**.

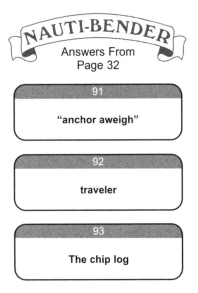

NAUTI-BENDER
Answers From Page 32

91

"anchor aweigh"

92

traveler

93

The chip log

Sailing behind an isolated thunderstorm, there will be _____ wind.

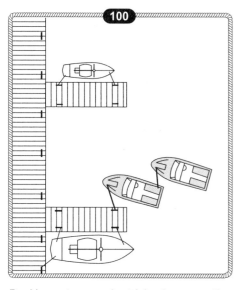

Docking a tow can be tricky; however, the method shown above enables the tug to push ahead, go astern to _____ her (without changing the bow line), or turn and nudge the stern in with her bow.

In heavy weather, a boat should be headed _____ or _____ _____ _____ the waves.

When fog begins to develop – after slowing down, posting lookouts, etc., the next most important step is to _____ your position (in the above, keep a sharp lookout; others may have the same idea).

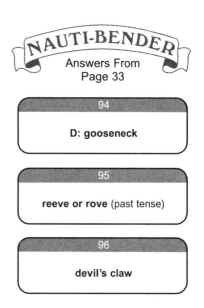

NAUTI-BENDER
Answers From
Page 33

94

D: gooseneck

95

reeve or rove (past tense)

96

devil's claw

Most survivors of crew-overboard situations credit their good fortune to **staying calm** and **keeping positive mental attitude** while conserving personal _____, maximizing _____, and conserving body _____.

NAUTI-BENDER
Answers From
Page 34

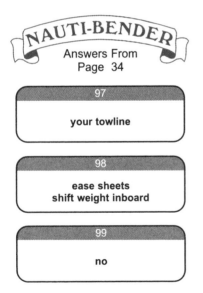

97

your towline

98

**ease sheets
shift weight inboard**

99

no

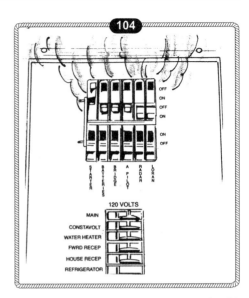

_____ fire extinguishers or water should **not** be used in electrical fires because they both conduct electricity.

Removing which element of the "fire triangle": **fuel**, **heat**, or **oxygen**, will extinguish the fire?

A safety harness is only as good as its attachment point. Life lines, sheets, stanchions, and pulpits are examples of **good** or **poor** attachments.

Before swimming off a boat or recovering a waterskier, **always** stop the engine and put it in _____ to prevent any further prop movement.

Safety tip: most experienced seamen never get underway at night without a _____ or pocket-size _____ _____ on their person.

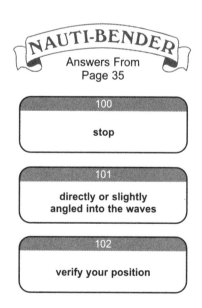

NAUTI-BENDER

Answers From
Page 35

100
stop

101
directly or slightly angled into the waves

102
verify your position

Three things to remember before launching the boat: disconnect trailer lights, secure dock lines to boat and make sure the _____ _____ has been put in!

The maximum speed that a displacement boat can make is governed by her _____ _____.

NAUTI-BENDER
Answers From Page 36

103
energy buoyancy heat

104
Foam

105
Any one of the three

Flag etiquette: at morning colors, the ensign is hoisted _____, before other flags. At evening colors, the ensign is lowered _____, with ceremony, after other flags.

Urgent radio communications regarding the safety of a vessel, person, or aircraft should be preceded by "_____-_____".

Identify the organizations the above flags represent. Which organization has law-enforcement authority?

VHF Communications: which of the following channels should be utilized for distress, safety, and calling transmissions: **13**, **16**, **22A**, **24**, **71** or **72**?

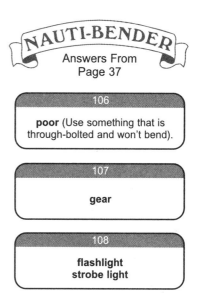

NAUTI-BENDER
Answers From
Page 37

106

poor (Use something that is through-bolted and won't bend).

107

gear

108

flashlight
strobe light

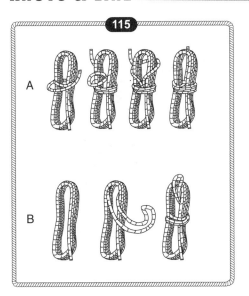

Halyards and lines should be routinely coiled in similar fashion for use in a hurry or at night. "**A**" above illustrates coiling a line for _____ and "**B**" for _____.

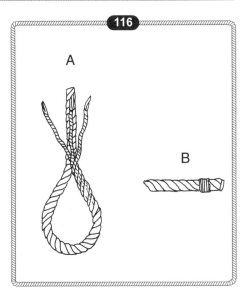

The way strands of rope are wound together is referred to as the: (A) **bend**, (B) **twist**, (C) **lay**, (D) **coil**.

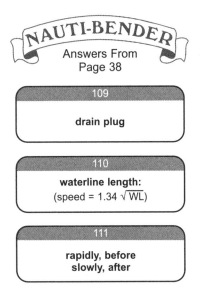

NAUTI-BENDER
Answers From
Page 38

109

drain plug

110

waterline length:
(speed = $1.34 \sqrt{WL}$)

111

rapidly, before
slowly, after

A tight kink in a line may reduce the line's strength by **15**, **30**, or **45%**.

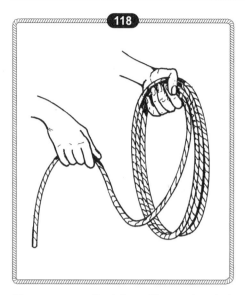

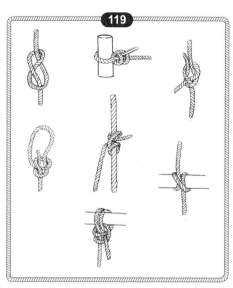

The proper method for coiling a stranded line (right-handed lay) would be in a _____ fashion.

A line is tied to itself by a _____. A _____ is typically used to fasten a line to another line. A _____ is used to fasten a line to an object.

Depending on the boat's configuration, you may be able to protect your boat during a lightning storm by clamping a length of chain to the bottom of the cap shroud and dropping the end in the _____.

NAUTI-BENDER
Answers From
Page 39

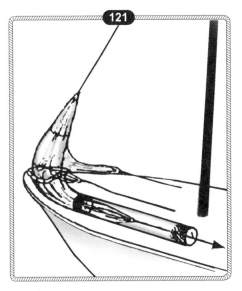

A tubular container located on the foredeck where the spinnaker is stowed is called the "_____ _____" or the "_____ _____".

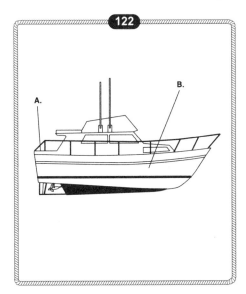

Hull language: "**A**" and "**B**" shown above would be referred to as the _____ and _____.

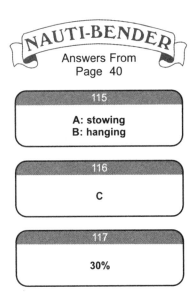

NAUTI-BENDER

Answers From
Page 40

115

A: stowing
B: hanging

116

C

117

30%

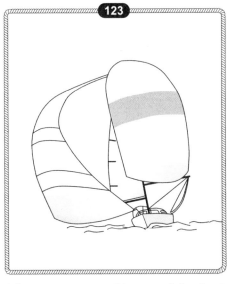

A "_____ or _____" is a very full sail set on the opposite side of the spinnaker.

"Telltales" and "Luff Yarns" are probably the best single aid to the helmsman and fly _____ to the sail when the boat is "_____" optimally.

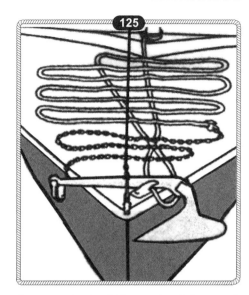

Anchor rode should be previously "_____" to facilitate free running when cast overboard.

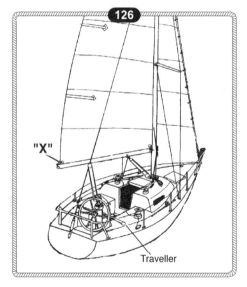

Sail Language: "**X**" shown above, would be referred to as the "_____" and is the control line system (mounted on the boom) used to control tension of the mainsail's "foot".

NAUTI-BENDER
Answers From Page 41

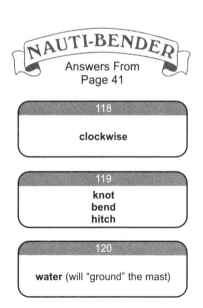

118
clockwise

119
knot
bend
hitch

120
water (will "ground" the mast)

"Sun Dog": a halo around the sun or moon will accurately forecast rain about _____ percent (sun) and _____ percent (moon) of the times viewed.

The wind's direction is said to "veer" when it shifts **clockwise** or **counter-clockwise** (typically after a front passes). The true wind is said to "_____" when its' speed increases.

NAUTI-BENDER
Answers From
Page 42

121
sally sock
chute or spinnaker scoop

122
A: transom
B: topsides

123
blooper or bigboy

When the tide is rising or "coming in", it is properly referred to as "_____"?

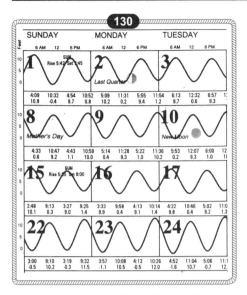

Typically, corresponding tides will occur approximately _____ minutes later on the following day.

When the wind picks up and white caps are beginning to form, what is the approximate wind speed?

When the tide is falling or "going out", it is properly referred to as "_____".

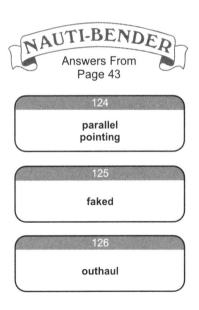

NAUTI-BENDER
Answers From Page 43

124

parallel
pointing

125

faked

126

outhaul

A "bow eye" is typically the strongest attachment point on a boat – excellent for attaching a _____ _____ or mooring _____.

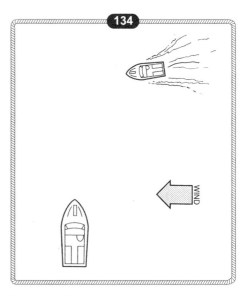

You are about to take a disabled vessel (shown above) in tow; she appears to have more leeway than your vessel. To pass the tow rope you should approach from: **off the port bow**, **off the starboard bow**, or **from head-on.**

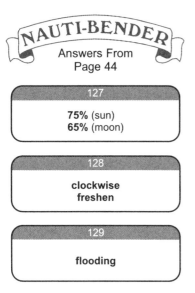

In a crew-overboard situation, in what order would you do the following: (A) **never lose sight of the victim**, (B) **toss a PFD**, (C) **radio in a mayday**, (D) **execute a Williamson turn**.

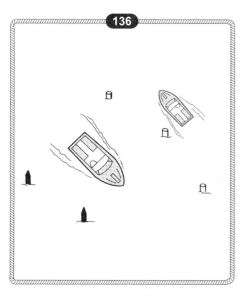

In some circumstances (thick fog, heavy ship traffic, etc.) it may be wise to run just _____ the edge of a well buoyed, deep-draft ship channel.

Assuming the sails are set and trimmed properly, as the vessel luffs from beam-reach to close-hauled, the apparent wind will move **forward** or **aft**.

Usually, the softest ride is achieved by running _____ the wind in rough weather.

NAUTI-BENDER
Answers From
Page 45

130
50 minutes

131
15 – 18 mph

132
ebbing

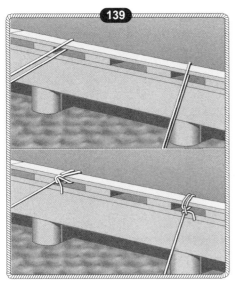

Tying up to a dock utilizing a "rail" system can be accomplished by running a line around the rail, then back to and cleated at the docking vessel; or by tying a _____ hitch followed by a _____ hitch.

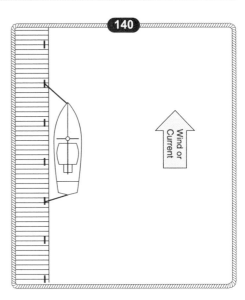

When departing, with your stern into tide or current (as shown above): you should leave **bow** or **stern** first.

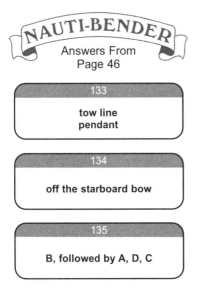
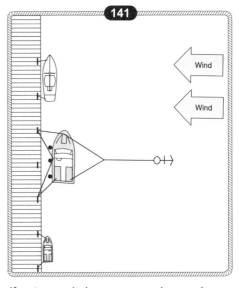

If a strong wind, waves, or wakes are banging your boat against the dock... set an anchor amidships, rig a bridle from the bow and stern and "_____" her away from the dock.

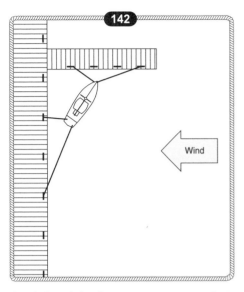

A windward berth may prove uncomfortable for overnight crew; if space permits, moor across a corner with lines _____ so the boat stays away from the sides.

At crowded marinas, open cleats are rare. So as not to disturb your neighbor's lines and vice versa, simply run your lines under the neighbor's lines and secure with a _____ as shown above.

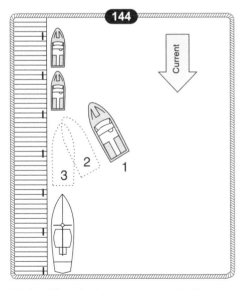

To "walk" a single-screen vessel sideways into a tight slip (assuming fairly strong current) hold steady against current by _____ the throttle while easing bow over.

NAUTI-BENDER
Answers From
Page 47

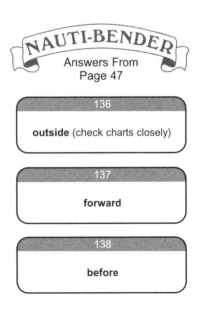

136

outside (check charts closely)

137

forward

138

before

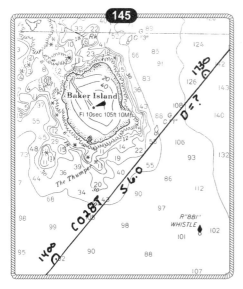

How far would you travel in 3 hours and 30 minutes cruising at 6 knots?

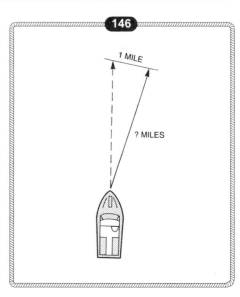

A 5 degree course error will result in being one mile off course after sailing **5.7, 8.2**, or **11.5** miles?

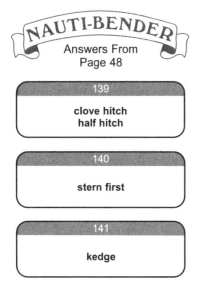

NAUTI-BENDER
Answers From
Page 48

139
clove hitch **half hitch**

140
stern first

141
kedge

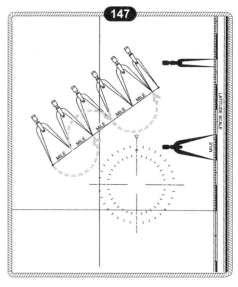

The distance shown by one minute of latitude equals _____ nautical mile(s) on the associated chart.

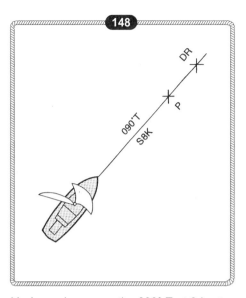

You're underway on the 090° T at 8 knots. After two hours, you are on your track line but two miles behind your DR. What's the set and drift of the current?

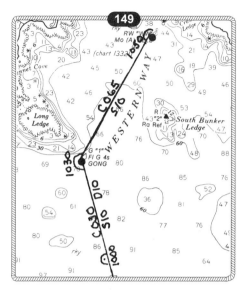

Even with excellent electronics and good weather, a DR or Dead Reckoning Plot should be maintained and logged when: (A) **changing speed**, (B) **changing course**, (C) **at least once an hour**, (D) **when taking a bearing**, or (E) **all of the above.**

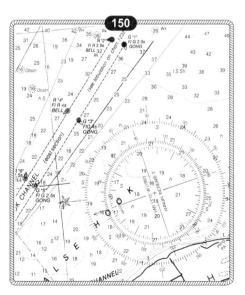

What compass course would you steer going from buoy **G "5"** to **G "1"**?

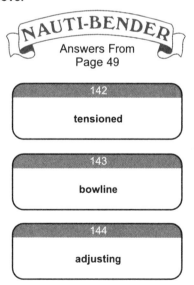

NAUTI-BENDER
Answers From
Page 49

142

tensioned

143

bowline

144

adjusting

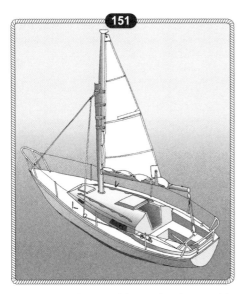

151

In most equipment failure situations, with the materials on board and the sailor's inventiveness, the problem can be temporarily "_____- _____", enabling continued passage.

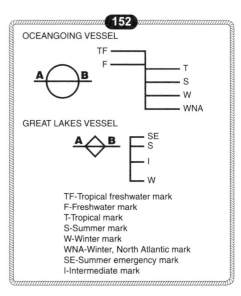

152

OCEANGOING VESSEL

GREAT LAKES VESSEL

TF-Tropical freshwater mark
F-Freshwater mark
T-Tropical mark
S-Summer mark
W-Winter mark
WNA-Winter, North Atlantic mark
SE-Summer emergency mark
I-Intermediate mark

"Plimsoll mark": the letters shown on either side of the circle or diamond indicate the issuing load line authority. In the above example, "**A**", "**B**", indicates _____ _____ _____ _____ _____.

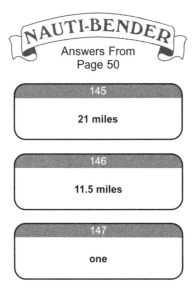

NAUTI-BENDER
Answers From Page 50

145

21 miles

146

11.5 miles

147

one

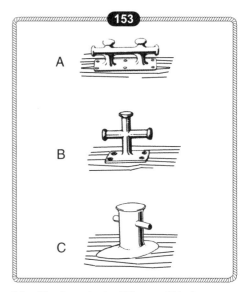

153

A

B

C

Identify the dock fittings: **(A)** "_____ _____", **(B)** "_____ _____", and **(C)** "_____" shown above.

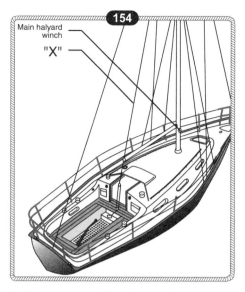

Main halyard winch

"X"

Sail Language: "**X**", shown above, would be referred to as the _____ _____.

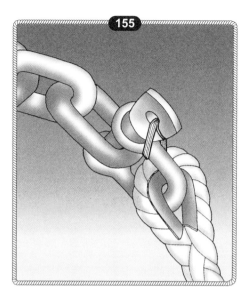

After mooring or anchor-rode shackles have been tightened, "_____" the shackle pin with copper wire, small stuff, or a plastic tie wrap.

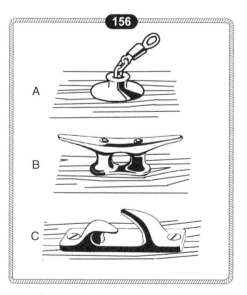

A

B

C

Identify the deck gear shown above: "**A**" _____ _____, "**B**" _____ and "**C**" _____.

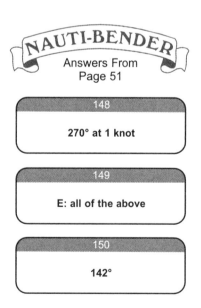

NAUTI-BENDER
Answers From
Page 51

148
270° at 1 knot

149
E: all of the above

150
142°

The color of the evening sky can be a good indicator of the next day's weather. A yellow sunset typically means _____ winds, especially at midday.

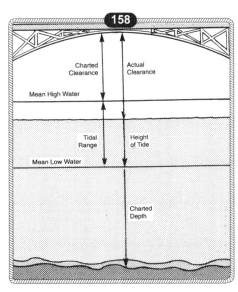

In area's of semi-diurnal tides, there are typically _____ tides per day.

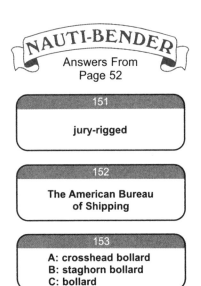

NAUTI-BENDER
Answers From Page 52

151

jury-rigged

152

The American Bureau of Shipping

153

A: crosshead bollard
B: staghorn bollard
C: bollard

Generally speaking, the most destructive storms occuring on the Great Lakes usually come from the: **Northeast/East**, **Southwest/West**, **Northwest/North**, or **Southeast/South**?

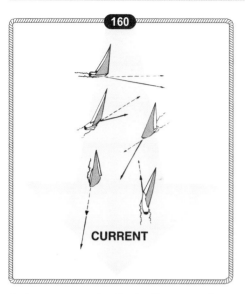

160

CURRENT

A beam current affects the **speed** or **course** made good over the ground?

161

Wind direction can be most accurately esti-mated by observing the: **swells**, **waves**, **cloud movement** or **none of the above**.

162

Current runs **faster** or **slower** in deep water and **faster** or **slower** in shallow water.

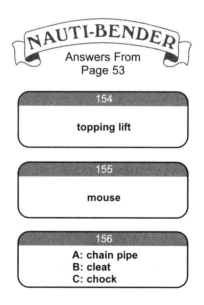

NAUTI-BENDER
Answers From
Page 53

154
topping lift

155
mouse

156
A: chain pipe B: cleat C: chock

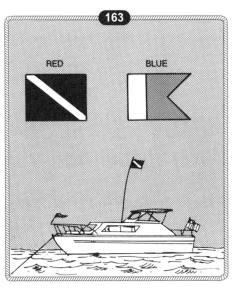

When you observe a diver's flag, you're required to keep _____ feet away from the diver's vessel.

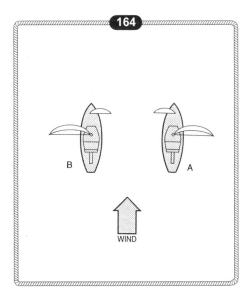

As shown above, which boat has the right of way or is the "stand-on vessel"?

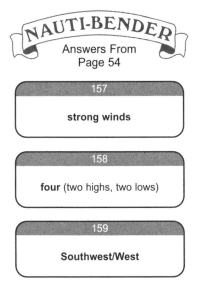

NAUTI-BENDER
Answers From Page 54

157

strong winds

158

four (two highs, two lows)

159

Southwest/West

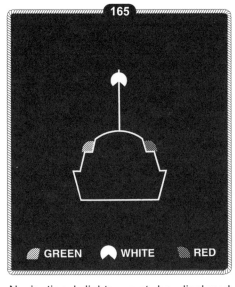

GREEN   WHITE   RED

Navigational lights must be displayed between _____ and _____ or in times of restricted visability.

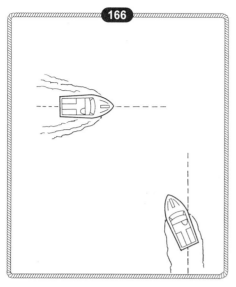

166

In a crossing situation, when does the "stand-on" vessel take action?

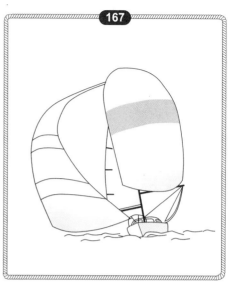

167

Most recreational boats utilize main and jib sails of _____ and spinnakers made of _____.

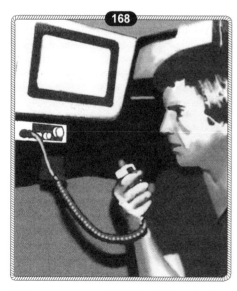

168

After an unsuccessful attempt at contacting another boat on Channel 16, you should wait _____ minutes before another attempt, and after three attempts wait _____ minutes before resuming.

NAUTI-BENDER

Answers From
Page 55

160

course

161

waves

162

faster (deep water)
slower (shallow water)

169

Cardinal buoys (typically used in Canada) indicate the _____ or _____ water by reference to the "cardinal" points of the compass.

170

A red and _____ combination or spherical buoy is used to mark a fairway or midchannel.

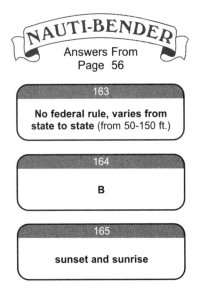

NAUTI-BENDER
Answers From
Page 56

163

No federal rule, varies from state to state (from 50-150 ft.)

164

B

165

sunset and sunrise

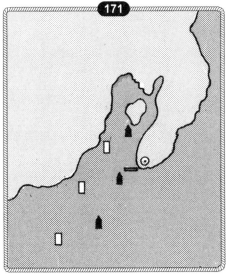

171

The number sequence on buoys **increase** or **decrease** from seaward?

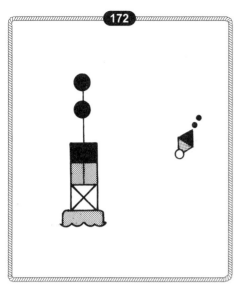

Buoys with red and black bands indicate
_____.

The vessel above is displaying a day
shape, indicating she is under _____.

Green daymarks have a _____ shape
since the silhouette resembles the top of a
_____ buoy and are _____ numbered.

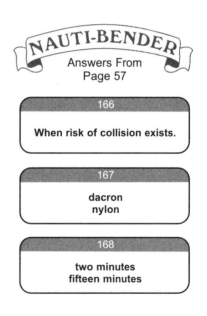

Wind will have the most effect on a vessel when she is: **backing down**, **going slow ahead**, **going full ahead** or **turning**.

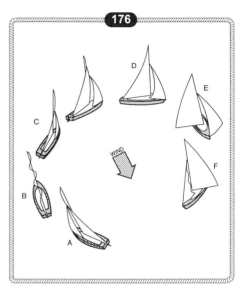

The center board does not have to be down when: **beating**, **running**, or **reaching**.

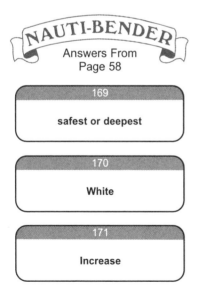

NAUTI-BENDER
Answers From
Page 58

169

safest or deepest

170

White

171

Increase

When proceeding up a shallow channel or inland river, as bottom approaches the boats normal draft a "suction" effect may cause the stern to "_____" and cause the boat to unexpectedly run aground.

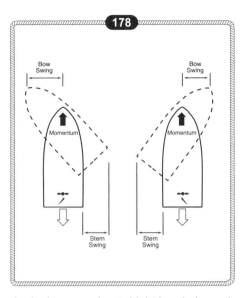

A single-screw boat (right-handed prop) will have more stern swing when turning **left** or **right**?

Hard-chined sailboats sail **faster** or **slower** with the chines buried?

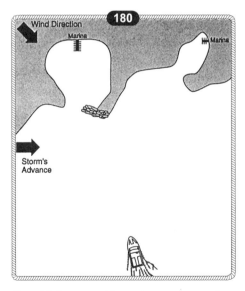

Caught in a sudden storm, one option would include _____ in the lee of an island or point of land.

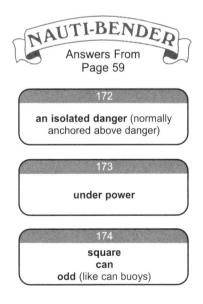

NAUTI-BENDER
Answers From Page 59

172

an isolated danger (normally anchored above danger)

173

under power

174

square
can
odd (like can buoys)

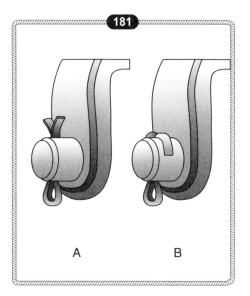

181

A   B

Is the proper method of securing a cotter pin shown in "**A**" or "**B**" above?

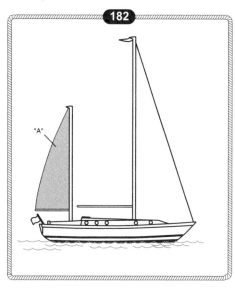

182

"A"

The sail indicated in "**A**" above is referred to as the "_____".

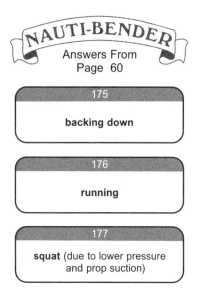

NAUTI-BENDER
Answers From Page 60

175

backing down

176

running

177

squat (due to lower pressure and prop suction)

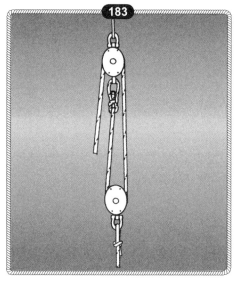

183

A line rove through blocks forms a "_____".

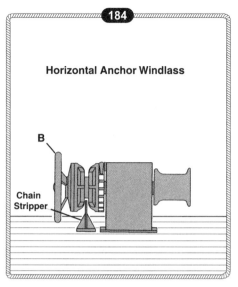

Windlass Nomenclature: "**B**" shown above is referred to as the "_____" which is used to increase or decrease pressure on the chain.

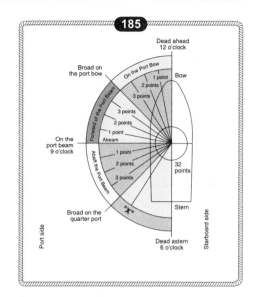

Language under way: an object bearing at point "**X**" (shown above) would be referred to as _____ _____ _____ _____ _____ _____.

Multi-hulled sail or powerboats are referred to as a "_____" or a "_____".

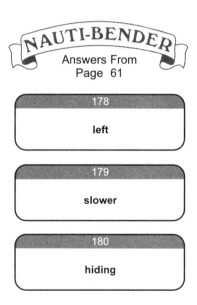

NAUTI-BENDER
Answers From
Page 61

178

left

179

slower

180

hiding

A boat will float **lower**, **the same**, or **higher** in fresh versus saltwater?

The water-ski hand-signal shown above indicates _____.

NAUTI-BENDER
Answers From
Page 62

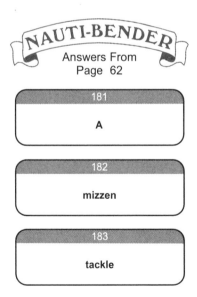

181

A

182

mizzen

183

tackle

Hey Charlie... catching any?

Radio transmissions between boats should be of the minimum length possible... not to exceed **three-**, **five-**, or **seven-minutes**.

The average recreational boater spends _____ to _____ hours cruising per year under power.

Inveterate sailors proclaim for a vessel to be "lucky" she should be named after: **a bird**, **a fish**, **the captain's significant other**, or **a famous place** (pick two).

The best way to climb out of the water into a dinghy is over the transom, with another crew member forward acting as a _____.

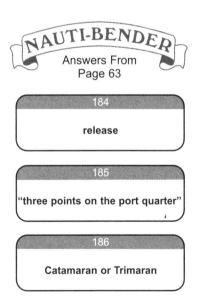

NAUTI-BENDER
Answers From
Page 63

184
release

185
"three points on the port quarter"

186
Catamaran or Trimaran

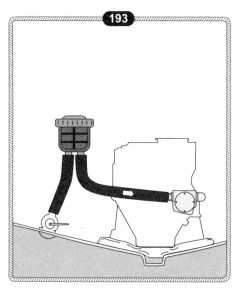

193

To avoid pumping oil or other contaminants overboard via the bilge pump, you may want to consider placing a bilge "_____" under your engine(s).

194

Are your lexan or plexiglas windows/windshield getting cloudy? Avoid using household glass cleaners. They typically contain _____, which reacts badly to plastic.

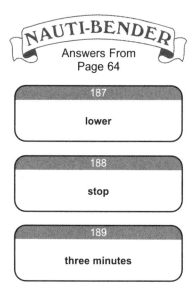

NAUTI-BENDER
Answers From Page 64

187

lower

188

stop

189

three minutes

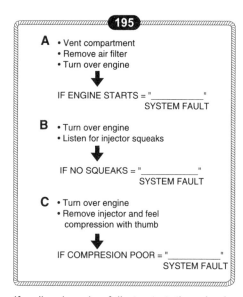

195

A
• Vent compartment
• Remove air filter
• Turn over engine

↓

IF ENGINE STARTS = "_____"
SYSTEM FAULT

B
• Turn over engine
• Listen for injector squeaks

↓

IF NO SQUEAKS = "_____"
SYSTEM FAULT

C
• Turn over engine
• Remove injector and feel compression with thumb

↓

IF COMPRESION POOR = "_____"
SYSTEM FAULT

If a diesel engine fails to start, three basic systems: **(A)**_____, **(B)**_____, and **(C)**_____ should be checked (as described above) until the fault is isolated.

When polishing and waxing nooks and crannies around the boat (especially hand rails), a _____ is a highly effective cleaning tool.

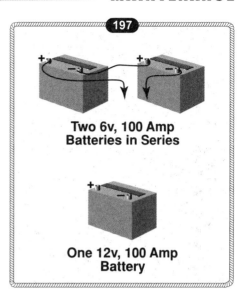

Two 6v, 100 Amp Batteries in Series

One 12v, 100 Amp Battery

Which battery configuration will provide more cranking power?

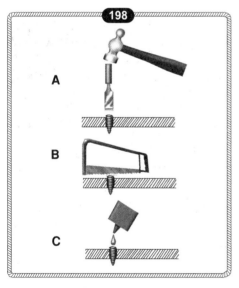

A

B

C

To remove a frozen screw with the head sheared off: (A) **bang smartly with a hammer**, (B) **cut (hacksaw) or chisel a slot in the remaining shank**, (C) **treat with "Liquid Wrench™"**, or (D) **all of the above**.

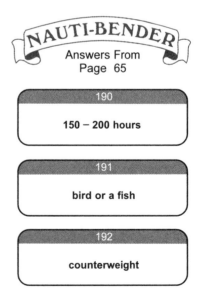

NAUTI-BENDER

Answers From
Page 65

190
150 – 200 hours

191
bird or a fish

192
counterweight

WHITE

The above vessel's light configuration would indicate she is _____.

In fog it is a practice to _____ your engine(s) at regular intervals and listen for fog signals.

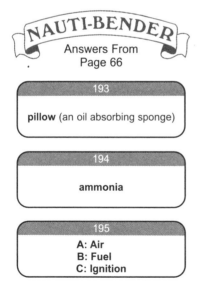

NAUTI-BENDER
Answers From
Page 66

193

pillow (an oil absorbing sponge)

194

ammonia

195

A: Air
B: Fuel
C: Ignition

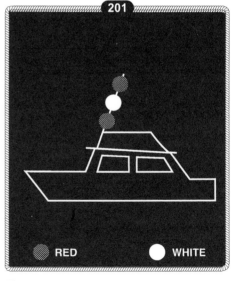

RED   WHITE

The above light configuration indicates a small vessel engaged in _____ operations.

A powerboat at anchor in restricted visibility should ring a bell for five seconds every minute or sound _____ blast(s).

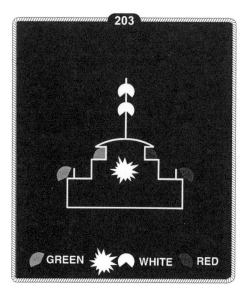

GREEN ✦ WHITE RED

The four standard colors used for lighted aids to navigation are **red**, **green**, **white** and _____.

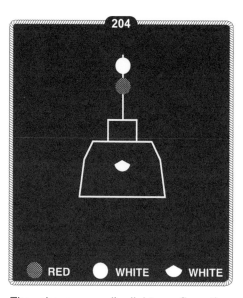

RED WHITE WHITE

The above vessel's light configuration would indicate she is a _____ _____.

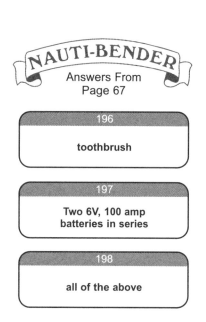

NAUTI-BENDER
Answers From Page 67

196
toothbrush

197
Two 6V, 100 amp batteries in series

198
all of the above

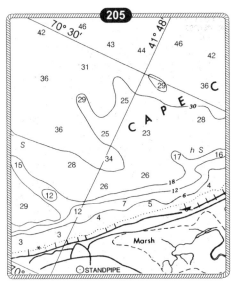

205

Horizontal or **vertical** lines on a nautical chart are called "parallels of latitude" ("lat is flat") and are the angular measurement of distance _____ and _____ of the equator.

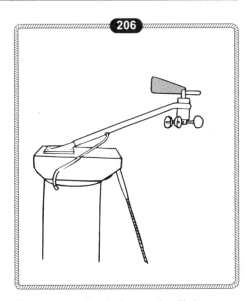

206

The apparent wind speed will be zero when: the true wind is from dead **ahead** or **astern** and equals the _____ speed.

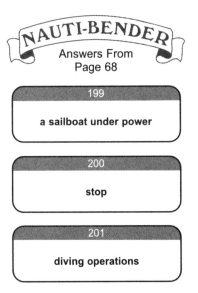

NAUTI-BENDER
Answers From
Page 68

199
a sailboat under power

200
stop

201
diving operations

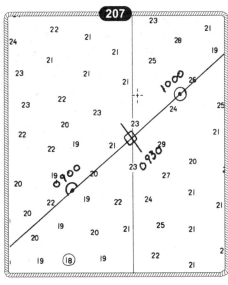

207

When logging positions on chart, universal symbols are used: identify "**A**" **(0900)**, "**B**" **(0930)** and "**C**" **(1000)**, in the above (shown for illustrative purposes only).

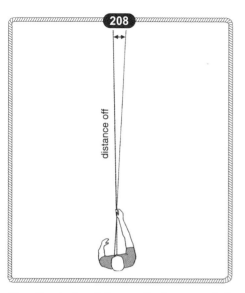

208

To estimate the distance off: close your left eye, line up a pencil as shown above, open left eye and close right. Estimate and multiply the distance the pencil has apparently moved (feet, yards, miles) by _____.

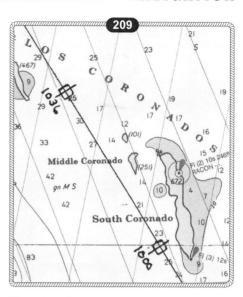

209

The six minute rule: states that a vessel will travel one-tenth her speed (in distance) in six minutes. Applying this rule: how far will a 10-knot vessel travel in 36 minutes?

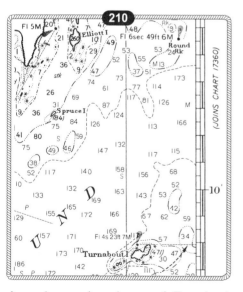

210

(JOINS CHART 17360)

Assuming you're abeam of Turnabout Island at 1000 hrs., what cruising speed would be required to reach Round Rock Light by 1100 hrs.?

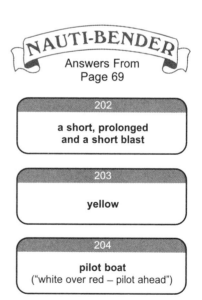

NAUTI-BENDER

Answers From
Page 69

202

**a short, prolonged
and a short blast**

203

yellow

204

pilot boat
("white over red – pilot ahead")

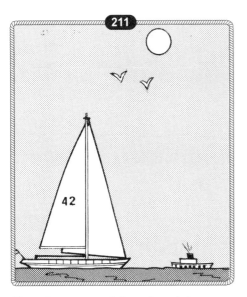

The above vessel is referred to as a "_____".

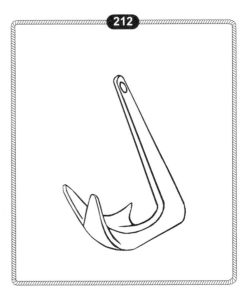

The "_____" anchor is good for most bottoms and well suited to hanging from a _____.

NAUTI-BENDER
Answers From
Page 70

205

horizontal
north and south

206

astern
vessel's

207

A. dead reckoning position
B. estimated position
C. fixed position

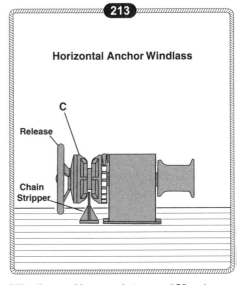

Horizontal Anchor Windlass

C

Release

Chain
Stripper

Windlass Nomenclature: "**C**" shown above is referred to as the "_____" which engages and hauls in the chain.

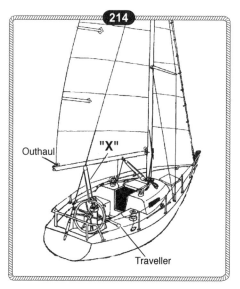

Outhaul

"X"

Traveller

Sail Language: "**X**" shown above would be referred to as the "_____" and is the primary line to control the _____ sail.

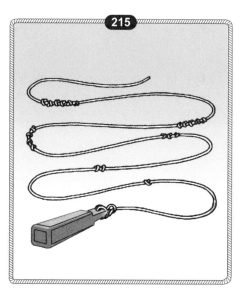

The "_____ _____", the traditional depth-measuring device, is cast ahead; when the boat catches up and the line runs vertical to the bottom, the knots (calibrated in feet or fathoms) indicate the depth.

"_____" boats cruise through the water vs. "_____" hulls that lift and skim over the water.

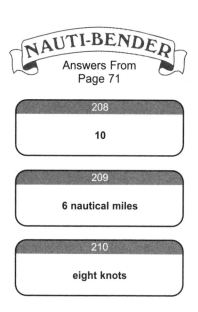

NAUTI-BENDER
Answers From
Page 71

208
10

209
6 nautical miles

210
eight knots

217

What is the first action a skipper should take if he/she senses fog is beginning to form?

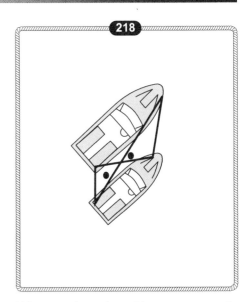

218

When towing alongside, your vessels maneuverability is greatly affected... acceleration will be **enhanced** or **reduced** and stopping ability will be **enhanced** or **reduced**.

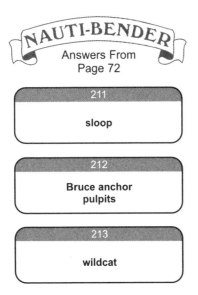

NAUTI-BENDER
Answers From
Page 72

211

sloop

212

Bruce anchor
pulpits

213

wildcat

219

Before rendering assistance to a disabled vessel, seriously consider the situation; if you are not experienced or otherwise equipped for the job – _____ _____ until qualified help arrives.

After running for 15-20 minutes, your outboard sputters and dies. The cause may be: **fouled plug(s)**, **out of gas**, **the fuel tank's vent is shut**, or **all of the above**.

The "_____ _____" shown above positions the crew farther away from the boat's center line, thus allowing more sail to be carried.

Never start an outboard or I/O engine dry or without a coolant water source. Just a few seconds of dry-operation can destroy the water-pump's _____.

NAUTI-BENDER
Answers From
Page 73

214
mainsheet **main sail**

215
lead line

216
displacement boats **planing hulls**

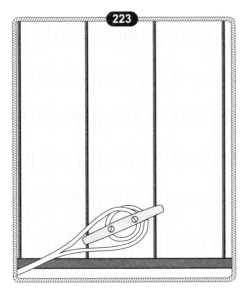

The above "belaying" technique is useful for _____ _____ handling; when ready, the slack line can be "flipped off" from on board.

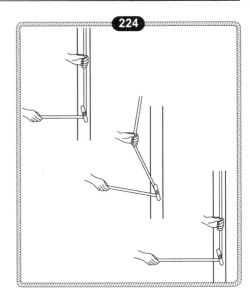

The above illustrates how a halyard or other lines can be hauled taut; this technique is referred to as "_____" or "_____-_____".

NAUTI-BENDER
Answers From Page 74

217
fix the vessel's position
(before landmarks/navigational aids are obscured)

218
acceleration reduced
stopping ability reduced

219
stand by

Which type of line has the greatest floatability characteristics: **nylon**, **dacron** or **polypropylene**?

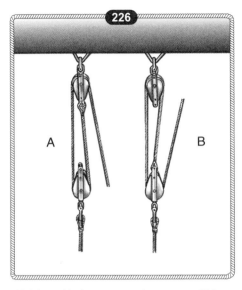

Which tackle is rove to advantage – "**A**", or "**B**", shown above?

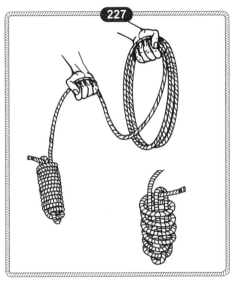

A "_____ _____" can be easily fashioned as shown above.

_____ rope is best suited for a painter or ski tow-line because its buoyancy characteristics will keep it out of the propeller(s) when backing down.

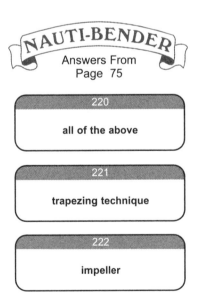

NAUTI-BENDER

Answers From
Page 75

220
all of the above

221
trapezing technique

222
impeller

A 1-1/2" hole located two feet below the water line will admit _____ gallons of water per minute... it has not been estimated how many gallons-per-minute a frightened man with a bucket may remove.

_____ sets of telltales (3-12 inches long, depending on boat's length) should be spaced evenly along the sail's luff and should be bright _____ or _____ for better visibility.

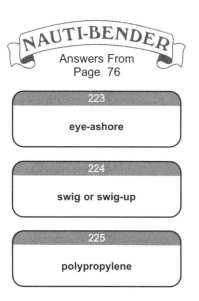

NAUTI-BENDER
Answers From
Page 76

223
eye-ashore

224
swig or swig-up

225
polypropylene

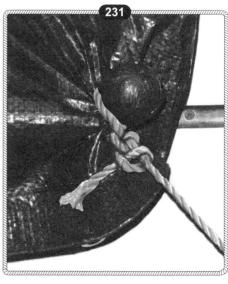

Want another year out of your boat cover? Where grommets have torn out, press an old golf ball against the inside of the cover, secure the outside with a _____ hitch followed by _____ hitches.

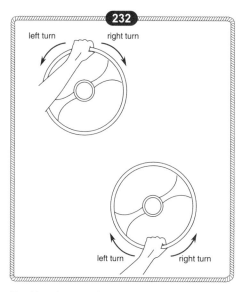

Backing boat trailers can be made easier by the placement of your hand on _____ of the wheel for going ahead and on the _____ for backing up (as shown above).

After colliding with another vessel, the penalty for failing to give aid without reasonable cause is _____ year(s) imprisonment or a $_____ fine.

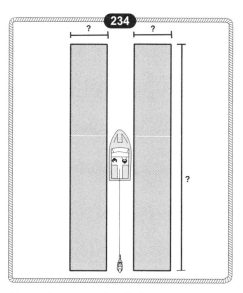

For safe waterskiing it is recommended that a _____-foot wide, unobstructed "ski corridor" at least _____ to _____-feet long be utilized.

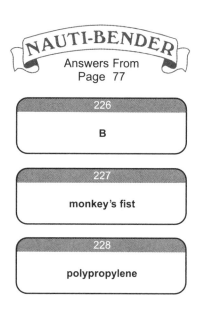

NAUTI-BENDER
Answers From
Page 77

226

B

227

monkey's fist

228

polypropylene

In reasonably _____ waters "seat cushion" PFD's can be rigged as **temporary fenders** (where the dock configuration does not lend itself to using standard fenders).

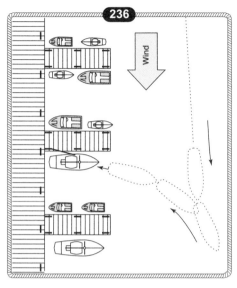

Docking in a leeward berth (assuming good reverse control): back in smartly and work _____ slow on the after bow spring until other lines are secured.

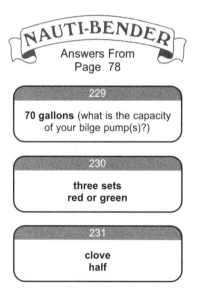

NAUTI-BENDER
Answers From
Page 78

229
70 gallons (what is the capacity of your bilge pump(s)?)

230
three sets
red or green

231
clove
half

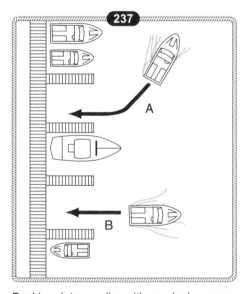

Backing into a slip with a single screw (right-handed prop) with no wind/current, approach "**A**" or "**B**" shown above, would be better?

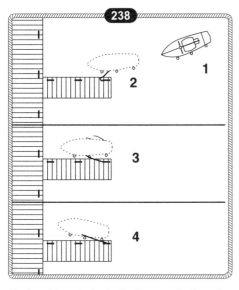

Spring Line Arrival: **1.** Approach the pier slowly at approximately a 20° angle; **2.** Neutral and attach spring; **3.** Back to stop boat's forward motion; **4.** Ahead slowly, rudder hard _____.

When entering a lock, be prepared for any mooring situation by having _____ and _____ rigged on both sides of the vessel.

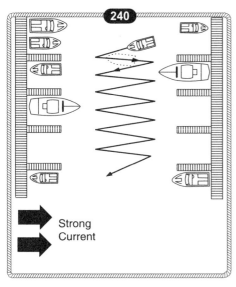

Strong
Current

To avoid being side-to the current and "_____ _____" onto the other boats, one should utilize a series of back and forth maneuvers.

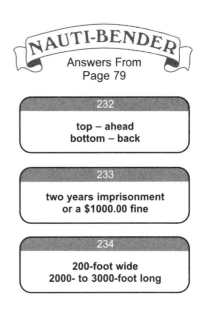

A pile of stones built in a symmetrcial or non-symmetrical form used as a navigational aid is referred to as a "_____".

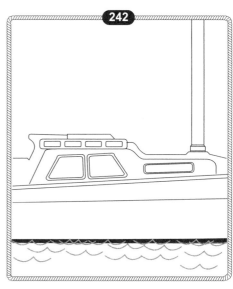

The raised area at the after end of a boat's cabin top is referred to as the "_____ _____".

NAUTI-BENDER
Answers From Page 80

235
calm (caution: compression reduces PFD's floatability)

236
ahead

237
A

"_____" is the error in the compass (usually different amounts East, West and so on)· caused by on-board ferrous materials or electronic equipment.

The downward curvature of the hawser between vessel towing and that being towed is referred to as the "_____".

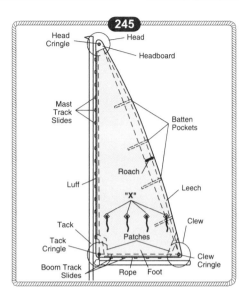

Sail Language: "**X**" (shown above) would be referred to as the "_____ _____".

What is the difference between "**pilings**" and "**dolphins**"?

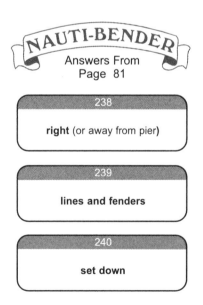

NAUTI-BENDER
Answers From
Page 81

238
right (or away from pier)

239
lines and fenders

240
set down

247

Makeshift or underrated _____ are less expensive and work **most** of the time.

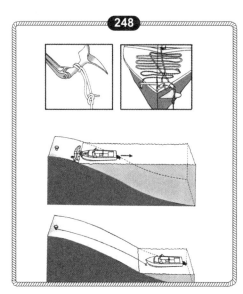

248

Anchoring and retrieving a boat in an ebb tide is easily accomplished by placing the anchor across the bow with the anchor rode faked behind, rigging a "_____ _____" to the anchor head, and proceeding as shown above.

249

When rafting, which boat should be anchored?

The proper maneuvering method when anchoring is to _____ _____ the wind or tidal flow (if stronger).

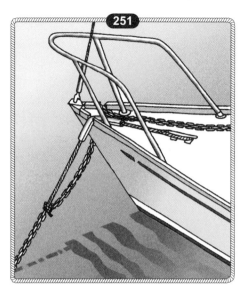

Boats with all-chain rodes should consider adding a nylon _____ _____ in bad weather, or while at rough anchorages.

Generally speaking, the most favorable bottom for anchoring is **soft mud**, **rocky**, a **mixture of mud and clay**.

NAUTI-BENDER
Answers From
Page 83

244
catenary

245
reef points

246
Dolphins are a cluster of pilings usually interconnected with cable.

Diesel oil, grease, or gasoline fires should be extinguished by: **dousing with water**, a **Type B**, or a **Type C extinguisher**.

In an emergency, diesel engines can be run completely underwater, provided the **fuel supply**, **battery** or **air intake** is above water?

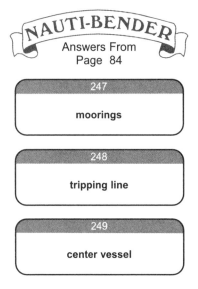

NAUTI-BENDER
Answers From
Page 84

247

moorings

248

tripping line

249

center vessel

In a crew-overboard situation it is important to assume a **H**eat **E**scape **L**essening **P**osture (H.E.L.P.) or "fetal" position since _____ percent of body heat is lost from the head.

"Fend off": to push a boat clear or prevent violent contact with another boat, dock or object either by using: (A) **hands/legs**; (B) **boat hook**; (C) **a fender**, or (D) **all of the above**.

On channel 16 "_____ _____" are reserved for distress, urgency and safety traffic during the _____ _____ after the hour and half-hour.

What danger exists to people when CO_2 is discharged in a confined area?

NAUTI-BENDER
Answers From
Page 85

250
head into

251
shock absorber

252
a mixture of mud and clay

259

Many boating accidents occur (especially at night) when a skipper unfamiliar with _____ _____ tries to pass between a tug (which may be utilizing up to a 1200' hawser) towing a barge.

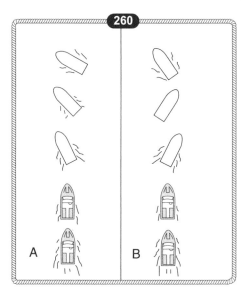

260

Going full-ahead with a single-screw vessel (right-hand propeller): if the engine is put astern with hard-left rudder the stern will: (A) **swing slowly, then quickly to port** or (B) **swing to starboard until headway is lost, then to port**.

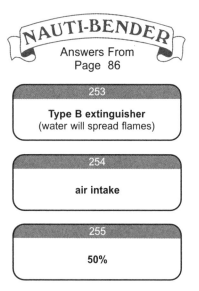

NAUTI-BENDER
Answers From
Page 86

253

Type B extinguisher
(water will spread flames)

254

air intake

255

50%

261

"_____ _____" is a yacht with the "forestay" attached to the masthead as opposed to a "_____ _____" where the "forestay" does not attach to the masthead.

When towing properly, the tow rope should be... **stretched tight**, **have some slack**, or should **dip in the wate**r.

Whether the vessel has a diesel or gas engine, it is always good practice, when starting, to check the exhaust to insure _____ _____ is coming out.

"Radial head" spinnakers are for use in _____ winds.

NAUTI-BENDER
Answers From
Page 87

256
B & C (very dangerous to use hands/legs)

257
**silent periods
three minutes**

258
suffocation

265

Docking under sail or with poor control in reverse can be challenging. In this situation, some skippers use a rugged bucket as a sea anchor to slow the boat's _____ _____.

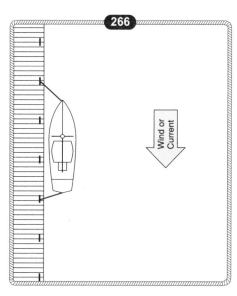

266

Wind or Current

When departing, with your bow into current (as shown above): you should leave **bow** or **stern** first.

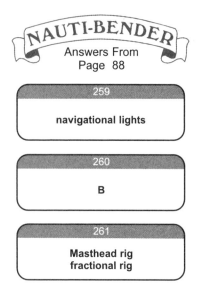

NAUTI-BENDER

Answers From
Page 88

259
navigational lights

260
B

261
Masthead rig **fractional rig**

267

When tying-up, run lines and/or position the boat to achieve a "_____ _____" through the chock to reduce chafing.

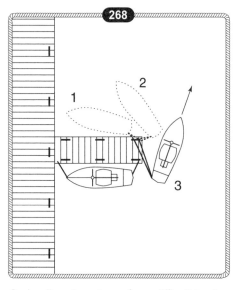

Spring-line departures from difficult berths can be made easier by rigging the spring as a "_____" line.

When docking with a strong wind or tide/current directly abeam, you must anticipate that the **bow** or **stern** will fall off first.

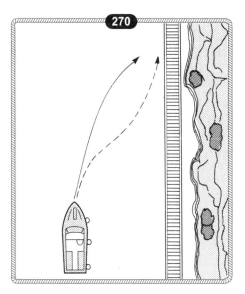

When docking a boat "side-to" with wind off the dock, the approaching turning angle should be **increased** or **decreased**?

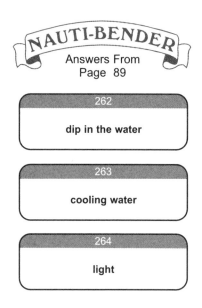

NAUTI-BENDER
Answers From
Page 89

262

dip in the water

263

cooling water

264

light

You discover a cracked fuel line and diesel is being sprayed on a hot engine. What should you do first: **declare a mayday, stand by with a fire extinguisher, shut off the fuel supply** or **secure the engine compartment**?

All boats, by law, must have a PFD for: **the stated maximum number of passengers**, **the usual number of passengers**, or **each person on board**?

NAUTI-BENDER
Answers From
Page 90

265
forward motion

266
bow first

267
fair lead

When conditions warrant wearing a safety harness, remember to snap on **before** going on _____ and keep on **at all times** while on _____.

If your vessel is in distress and your communications equipment and flare gun are inoperative, what are some other accepted distress signals: (A) **American flag flown upside down**; (B) **start smoky fire**; (C) **wave arms rapidly**; (D) and/or **continuous gun fire**?

The key to a successful rescue in a "crew-overboard" situation is: (A) **good communication**; (B) **a good crew**; (C) **the proper equipment made easily accessible**; (D) **regularly scheduled drills**.

In a crew overboard situation – where should the life ring/line be thrown: **behind and beyond**, **to the right**, or **in front of** the victim?

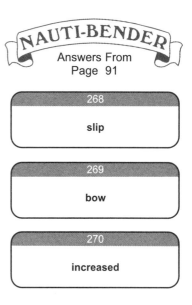

NAUTI-BENDER
Answers From
Page 91

268
slip

269
bow

270
increased

277

To easily find your way back to an unfamiliar harbor, channel, etc. – look _____ when departing and take mental images of the harbor entrance, buoys, landmarks etc..

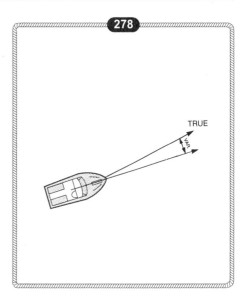

278

TRUE

VAR

TRUE bearings plus or minus variation amounts will equal _____ headings.

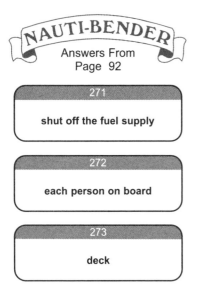

NAUTI-BENDER

Answers From
Page 92

271

shut off the fuel supply

272

each person on board

273

deck

279

A tug pushing a barge down the Mississippi River would measure the trip in "_____" miles.

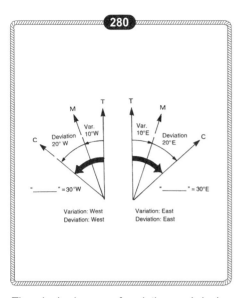

The algebraic sum of variation and deviation is referred to as "_____ _____".

To convert knots into miles-per-hour: multiply knots by _____.

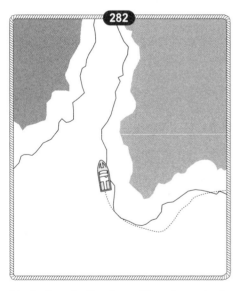

Navigating in the fog with only a depth sounder can be accomplished by "sounding" a course that follows an appropriate _____ _____ _____ on the associated chart.

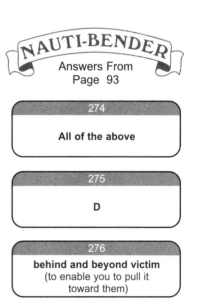

NAUTI-BENDER
Answers From Page 93

274

All of the above

275

D

276

behind and beyond victim
(to enable you to pull it toward them)

Sea breezes (close to shore) tend to **increase** or **decrease** in velocity as the day goes on?

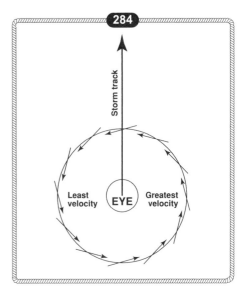

Tropical storms (wind 64K's plus) advance at speeds up to 25 knots with wind circulating _____ in the Northern Hemisphere and _____ in the Southern Hemisphere.

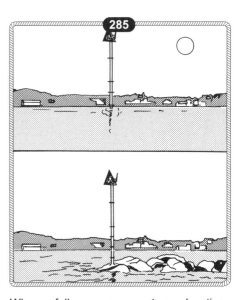

When a full moon occurs at your location, what time is high tide?

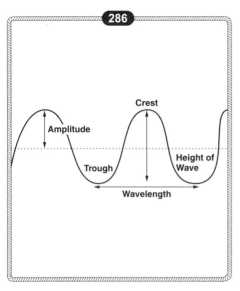

What are the three factors contributing to the height of a normal (non-seismic) wave?

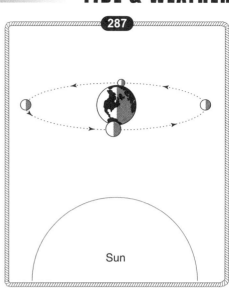

"Neap Tides" (lower highs, higher lows) occur twice a month on the _____ and _____ quarters of the moon.

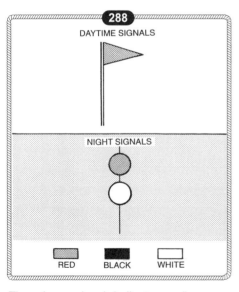

The above signal indicates a "_____-_____" weather warning with winds between _____-_____ knots.

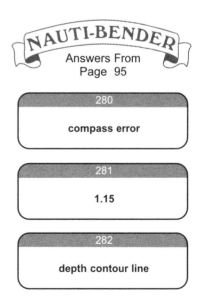

NAUTI-BENDER
Answers From
Page 95

280
compass error

281
1.15

282
depth contour line

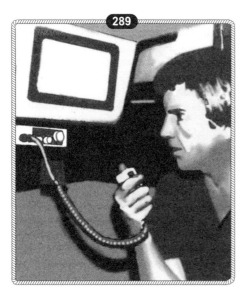

289

Which word(s) should be used preceding a VHF announcement about dangerous weather conditions: **"Mayday"**, **"Pan-Pan"**, **"Security"**, or **"Now hear this"**?

290

1. Avoiding alcoholic beverages
2. Avoiding greasy foods
3. Avoiding exhaust fumes
4. Keeping warm and dry
5. Staying on deck, amidships
6. Siting down
7. Drinking ginger ale
8. Keeping mentally and physically active (steer the boat)
9. Focusing on the horizon
10. Lying down or stand upright

Which of the above **does not** help prevent seasickness?

NAUTI-BENDER
Answers From
Page 96

283
Increase

284
counterclockwise – (northern)
clockwise – (southern)

285
Full-moon tides always occur at a specific location around the same hour ± 60 minutes

291

Personal watercraft are regarded as a _____ _____ motor vessel by the Coast Guard and therefore, must comply with **all** boating rules and requirements under federal law.

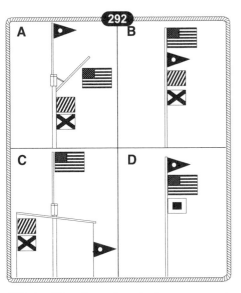

Which of the above flag displays represent proper flag etiquette?

Although your yacht club may not approve, the "_____ _____" system, shown above, is 99% effective (excluding fly-bys). Lash wind socks or pieces thereof to a length of small stuff and string fore to aft.

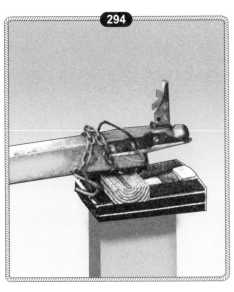

Boat Trailering: tongue weight should be between _____ to _____ percent of the GTW (**G**ross **T**railer **W**eight) – weight of trailer, boat, fuel, and cargo.

NAUTI-BENDER
Answers From
Page 97

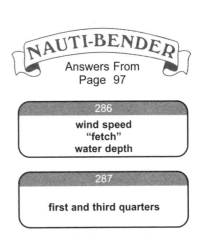

286
wind speed "fetch" **water depth**

287
first and third quarters

288
Small-craft 18-33 knots

When fog develops, lookouts should be posted both _____ and _____, especially in slower-moving vessels.

Proper "trim" can be achieved in the above boat by tilting the drive **back** or **forward**?

NAUTI-BENDER
Answers From Page 98

289
security
(pronounced say-cure-e-tay)

290
sitting down (worst position)

291
class "A" motor vessel
(16' or less/mech prop)

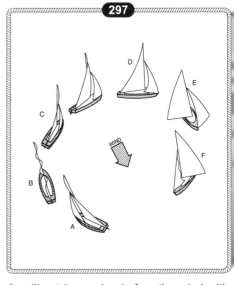

A sailboat is running before the wind with main full to the starboard and the jib full to the port ("E" above). This sailing method is referred to as "_____ and _____".

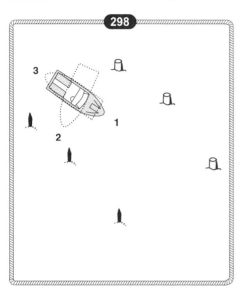

Going ahead on twin engines, what actions will turn the boat the quickest: (A) **reverse port engine, hard right rudder**; (B) **reverse starboard engine, rudder amidships**; or (C) **reverse starboard engine, hard right rudder**?

The quickest and safest way to shut down a runaway diesel engine is to cut off the (A) **air**, (B) **fuel**, or (C) **electrical** supply.

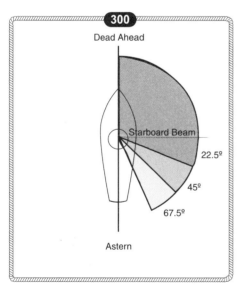

How many degrees abaft the beam of the vessel ahead must a boat be to be considered "overtaking": **22.5°**, **45°**, or **67.5°**?

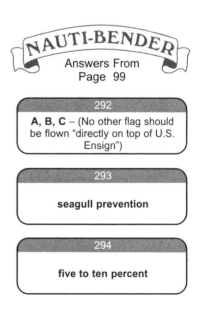

NAUTI-BENDER
Answers From
Page 99

292
A, B, C – (No other flag should be flown "directly on top of U.S. Ensign")

293
seagull prevention

294
five to ten percent

The above vessel is referred to as a "_____".

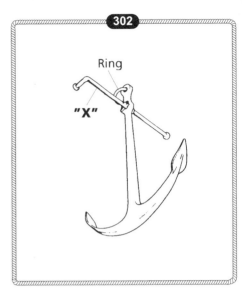

Anchor Nomenclature: "**X**" shown above would be referred to as the "_____".

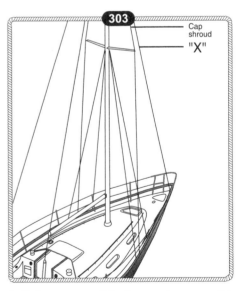

Sail Language: "**X**" shown above, would be referred to as the "_____".

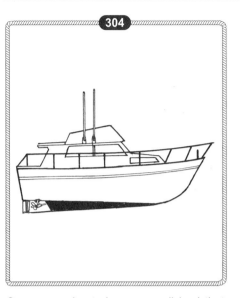

304

Some powerboats have a small keel that extends beyond and under the props called a "_____".

305

The "_____", a storage space at the stern of small craft sometimes utilized to house auxiliary power in sailing vessels.

306

To "_____" a vessel means to move it into a desired position by manipulating lines extended to shore, dock, another boat, etc..

NAUTI-BENDER
Answers From Page 101

298

C (reverse starboard engine, hard right rudder)

299

A: cut off the air (discharge CO_2 extinguisher into the air intake)

300

22.5°

The main difference between nylon and other polyester fiber ropes (dacron, terylene or duron) is that nylon will _____.

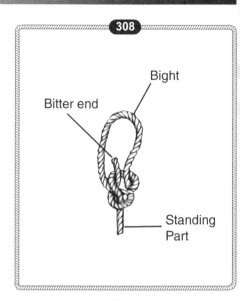

A bowline can easily be untied by simply working the **standing part**, **bitter end**, or **bight** toward the knot itself.

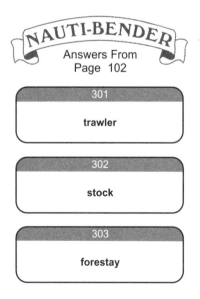

NAUTI-BENDER
Answers From
Page 102

301
trawler

302
stock

303
forestay

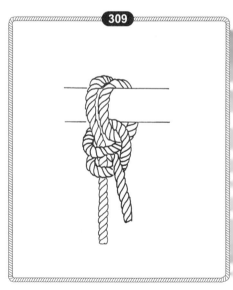

The "_____ _____" or fisherman's bend is used to secure a line to a buoy or to the ring of an anchor.

310

The "_____" or "square" knot is not recommended to lengthen lines and should be used sparingly.

311

Which line, assuming same diameter size, has more strength – **nylon** or **dacron**?

312

"_____" hitches and knots are useful in temporary situations and can be untied quickly, even under load.

NAUTI-BENDER
Answers From
Page 103

304
skeg

305
lazarette

306
warp

313

In fog a power vessel should sound a pro-longed blast at least once every _____ minutes.

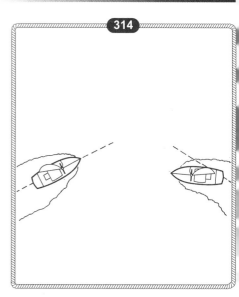

314

Sailboats under **power** or **sail** do not sound signals?

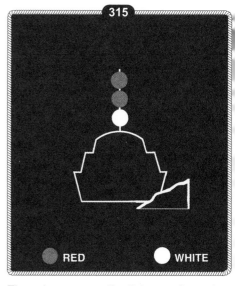

315

RED   WHITE

The above vessel's light configuration would indicate she is _____.

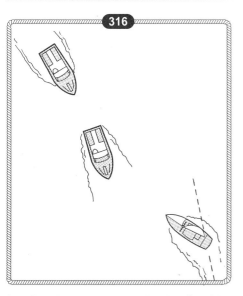

In a head-on or crossing situation (in sight visually) – to indicate "**I am going astern**", sound _____ blast(s).

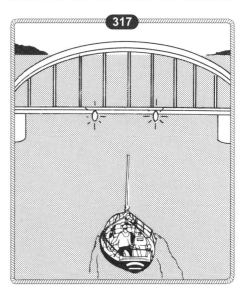

Red lights displayed under a single-span bridge indicate the _____ _____.

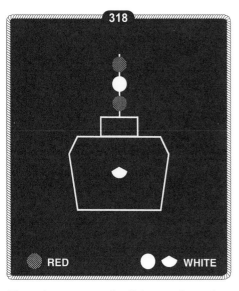

The above vessel's light configuration would indicate she is _____.

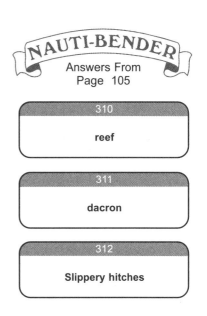

NAUTI-BENDER
Answers From
Page 105

310

reef

311

dacron

312

Slippery hitches

Smoke from exhaust (gasoline engine): if over-choked, or if a too rich fuel/air mixture exists, _____ smoke will be produced.

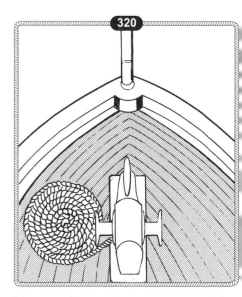

Many yachtsmen keep excess mooring lines looking neat on the deck by laying out the line in tight successive circles with the "bitter end" in the center – referred to as " _____ ".

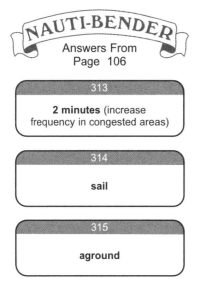

NAUTI-BENDER
Answers From
Page 106

313
2 minutes (increase frequency in congested areas)

314
sail

315
aground

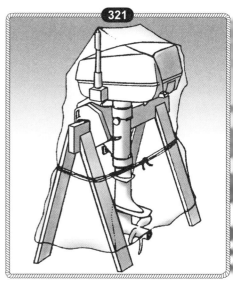

Outboard Motor Storage: motors should always be stored vertically so coolant water can drain. **Always** or **never** wrap motor tightly in plastic with duct tape to protect it over the winter.

Diesel Engine Performance: approximately 90 percent of engine problems emanate from _____ or _____ in the fuel.

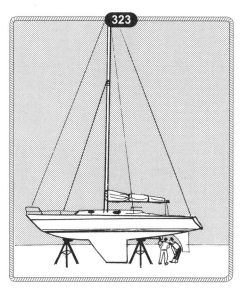

When winterizing your engine(s) (diesel or gas), it is a good practice to run the engine (without a coolant water source) until no water comes out of the exhaust – **true** or **false**.

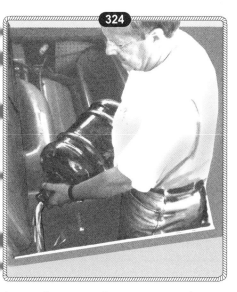

In a saltwater environment, to prolong a vessel's diesel or gasoline engine's life and minimize repairs, it is a good practice to _____ the engine with fresh water on a regular basis.

NAUTI-BENDER
Answers From Page 107

316

three short blasts

317

channel boundaries

318

restricted in maneuverability

The vessel above is displaying a day shape indicating she is _____.

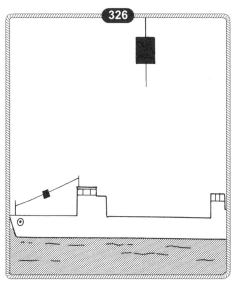

The vessel above is displaying a day shape indicating she is _____.

The above white buoy (with orange stripes) indicates?

Which of the following indicates a buoy that should be passed to port when entering from seaward: **white light**, **group flashing characteristic**, **a nun buoy**, or **an odd numbered buoy**?

The vessel above is displaying a day shape indicating she is _____ _____.

You are cruising 20-miles offshore. You observe a yellow flare off your starboard bow... what does this indicate?

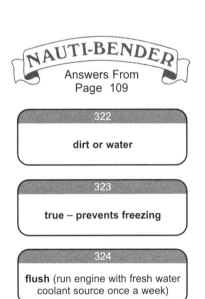

NAUTI-BENDER
Answers From
Page 109

322

dirt or water

323

true – prevents freezing

324

flush (run engine with fresh water coolant source once a week)

Boat Trailering: too little weight on the tongue will: (A) **have a tendency to pull up on the tow vehicle**; (B) **likely make the trailer "fishtale"**, and/or (C) **make the vehicle hard to steer**.

The clock shown above is indicating: 2 PM or _____ hours, and should be ringing _____ bells.

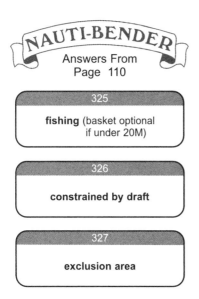

NAUTI-BENDER
Answers From
Page 110

325

fishing (basket optional if under 20M)

326

constrained by draft

327

exclusion area

Proper mooring pennant length ("L" above) is equal to **2.5**, **3.5** or **5** times the vertical distance from the water to topmost part of the bow.

334

The water-ski hand-signal shown above indicates: _____.

335

Sophisticated racing sails are typically made of _____ or _____.

336

What is the minimum weight of a vessel that can be "documented"?

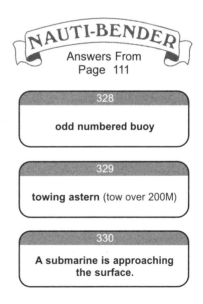

NAUTI-BENDER

Answers From
Page 111

328

odd numbered buoy

329

towing astern (tow over 200M)

330

A submarine is approaching the surface.

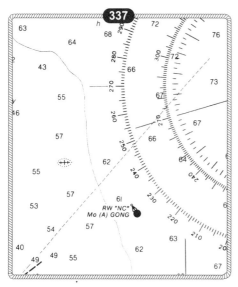

Referring to buoy symbol shown above: the line in the diamond indicates _____ _____; the little circle at the top indicates a _____ _____; and "GONG" indicates _____-_____ _____.

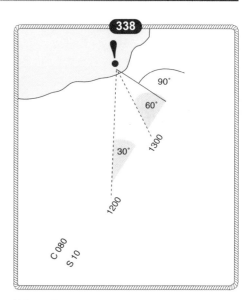

When directly abeam, what is the distance to the lighthouse (using "doubling on the bow" and the "seven-eighths" rule)?

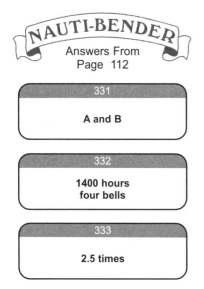

NAUTI-BENDER

Answers From
Page 112

331
A and B

332
1400 hours **four bells**

333
2.5 times

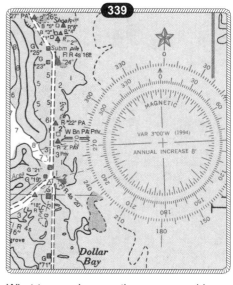

What true and magnetic course would you follow from light "**20**" to light "**24**"?

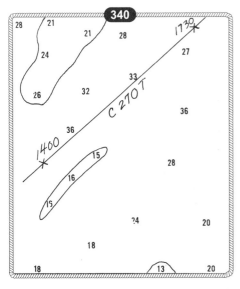

How far would you travel in 3 hours and 30 minutes cruising at 14 knots?

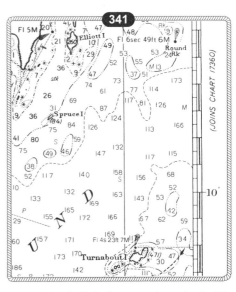

Round Rock Light is approximately **8**, **10**, or **11** nautical miles from Turnabout Island?

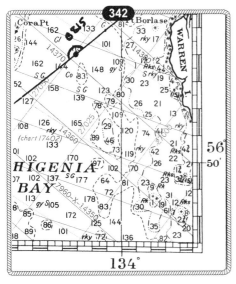

In the above example what is lat/lon position at 0815?

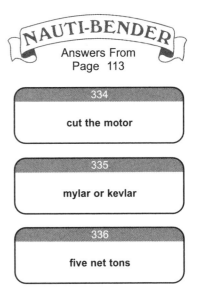

NAUTI-BENDER
Answers From
Page 113

334

cut the motor

335

mylar or kevlar

336

five net tons

343

To improve sailing performance while beating, the Captain should **ease** or **harden** the sheet line?

344

A vessel carrying sails with a low "aspect ratio" will perform better **close-hauled**, **broad-reaching** or **running**?

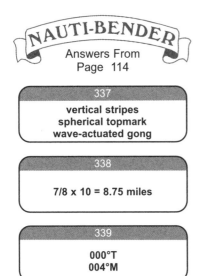

NAUTI-BENDER

Answers From
Page 114

337
vertical stripes **spherical topmark** **wave-actuated gong**

338
7/8 x 10 = 8.75 miles

339
000°T **004°M**

345

For a smoother ride in rough waters, maneuver in behind a larger vessel – stay within its wake to the right or left of the _____ _____.

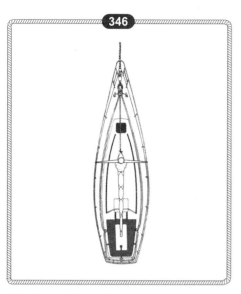

Most boats do not have heavy enough for-ward cleats for towing in rough seas. A double or trebled "_____ _____" should be rigged as shown above.

Before accepting a tow, discuss the situa-tion with your would-be rescuers – if they appear _____ or _____, you may be well advised to wait for qualified assistance.

Sailing at night, ahead you observe a large vessel with two white lights; the lower _____ light is seen to the left of the high-er _____ light. To avoid collision you should steer to the _____.

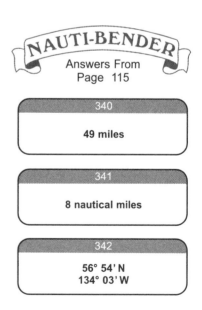

NAUTI-BENDER
Answers From
Page 115

340
49 miles

341
8 nautical miles

342
56° 54' N **134° 03' W**

349

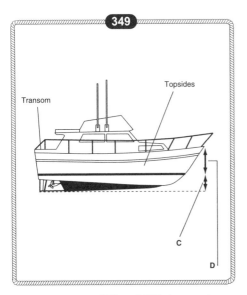

Transom

Topsides

C

D

Hull Language: "**C**" and "**D**" shown above would be referred to as the _____ and _____.

350

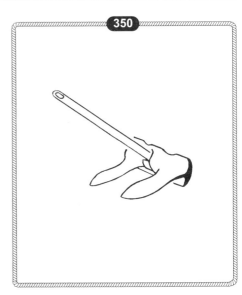

Although the _____ anchor comes in all sizes, it is best suited for _____ yachts.

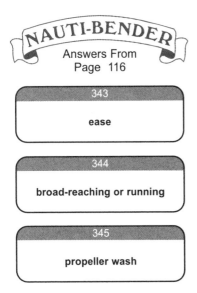

NAUTI-BENDER

Answers From
Page 116

343
ease

344
broad-reaching or running

345
propeller wash

351

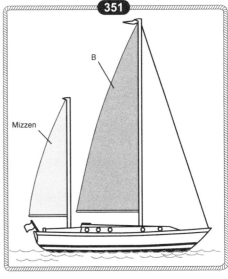

B

Mizzen

The sail indicated in "**B**" above is referred to as the _____.

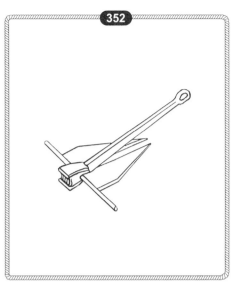

352

The _____, a modern anchor, holds **poorly**, **adequately**, or **well** in most bottoms.

353

When you "payout" or "slack" a mooring line under strain, it is referred to as "_____" the line.

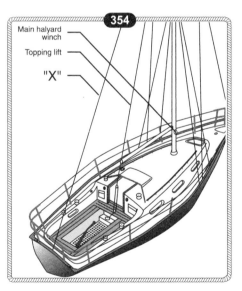

354

Main halyard winch

Topping lift

"X"

Sail Language: "**X**", shown above, would be referred to as the _____ _____.

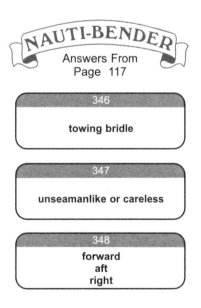

NAUTI-BENDER
Answers From
Page 117

346

towing bridle

347

unseamanlike or careless

348

forward
aft
right

The theoretical visibility of a lighthouse's light, in clear weather, depends on two factors: _____ and _____.

When there is probably loss of life or boat the universal emergency call "_____, _____, _____", should be used.

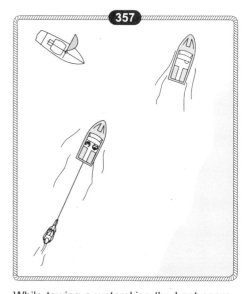

While towing a waterskier, the boat operator should maneuver to always keep the skier a distance equal to twice the _____ _____ length away from any potential hazards.

"Documented" vessels are required to display the vessel's name in _____ locations.

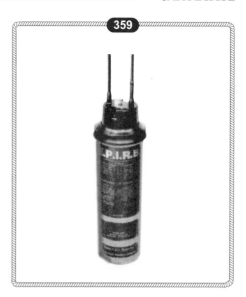

An EPIRB can send a signal as far as 200 miles, alerting passing _____ that an emergency exists, and will lead searchers to the distress scene.

Water-ski hand-signal shown above indicates: _____.

NAUTI-BENDER
Answers From
Page 119

352
Danforth holds well

353
surging

354
back stay

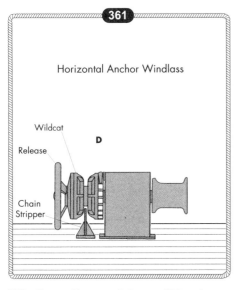

361

Horizontal Anchor Windlass

Wildcat

D

Release

Chain
Stripper

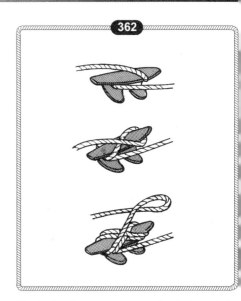

362

Windlass Nomenclature: "**D**", shown above, is referred to as the "_____ _____" which locks the wildcat, preventing the chain from running out.

Typically lines are properly fastened to dock cleats by a "_____ turn", a series of figure eights, and concluded with a half-hitch.

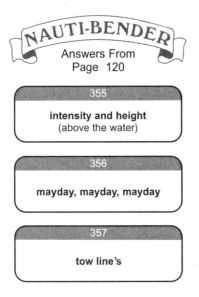

NAUTI-BENDER
Answers From Page 120

355

intensity and height
(above the water)

356

mayday, mayday, mayday

357

tow line's

363

The above vessel is referred to as a "_____".

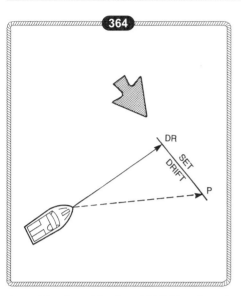

364

A combination of "set" and "drift" is referred to as "_____".

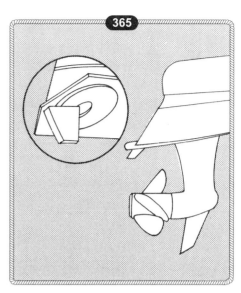

365

If it is hard to maintain a straight course at cruising speed, trim can be maintained by adjusting the transom drive's "_____ - _____", located under the activation plate.

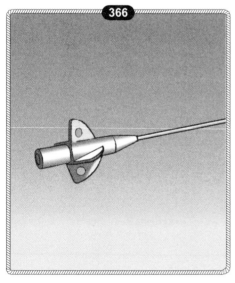

366

The patent log, a _____-measuring device, is towed and registers revolutions, recording in miles and tenths of a mile.

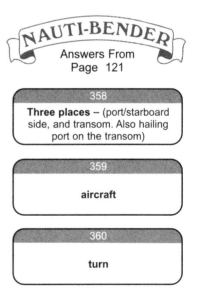

NAUTI-BENDER
Answers From
Page 121

358
Three places – (port/starboard side, and transom. Also hailing port on the transom)

359
aircraft

360
turn

Locking Strategy: when picking a spot to moor within a lock, try to avoid the gate ends where the _____ and _____ will be the strongest.

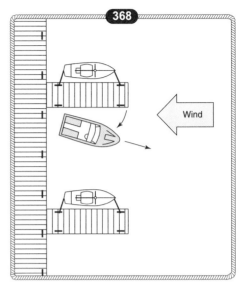

Departing head into wind: _____ the bow off and motor straight out.

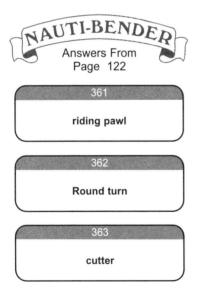

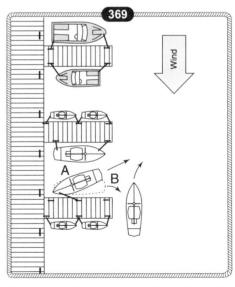

Departing Windward Berth: either "**A**" spring off the stern or "**B**" walk the boat to the end of the pier and motor off _____ the wind.

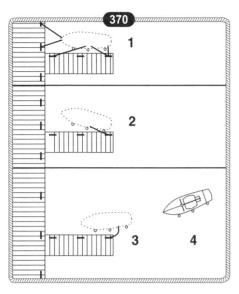

Spring Line Departure (strong wind or current): with all lines on, go ahead slow with rudder hard right. Cast off all lines except the _____ _____ _____, put engine in neutral, cast off spring, and back out normally.

The vessel shown above is docked head into a tidal flow or current. The boat can be temporarily held squarely alongside by a short, tight breast-line led from about _____ - _____ the distance from the bow.

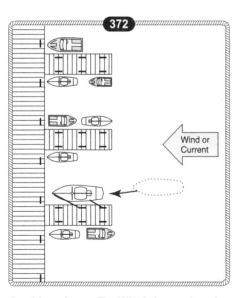

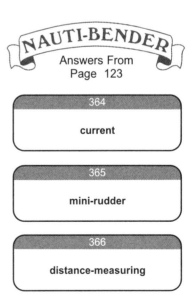

Docking Stern To Wind (assuming the vessel has poor reverse control): coast into the slip in neutral and slow the boat's forward momentum with the _____ spring and _____ line.

To safely waterski, it is recommended that a three-member team be used: _____, _____, and _____ _____.

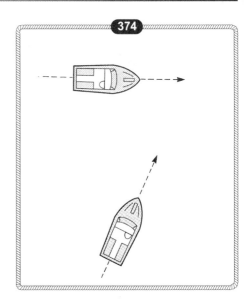

If in doubt between a "crossing" or "overtaking" situation, assume _____ and proceed accordingly.

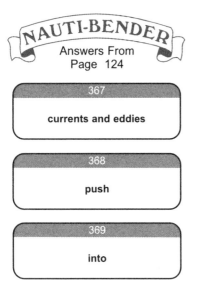

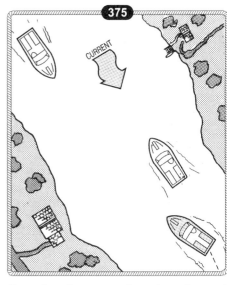

On a river the **up-** or **down**-bound vessel has the right-of-way?

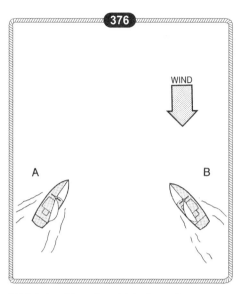

Which boat has the right-of-way?

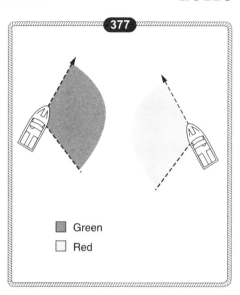

Green
Red

At night, the rule-of-thumb in a crossing situation is see red: _____ and see green: _____.

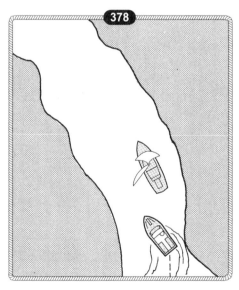

In an overtaking situation (**only** in narrow channels and **if** overtaken must take action), to indicate you are going to pass on the port, sound _____ blast(s).

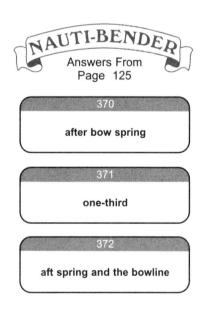

NAUTI-BENDER
Answers From
Page 125

370
after bow spring

371
one-third

372
aft spring and the bowline

379

If a vessel becomes "_____" or goes aground on a "spring" high tide, she may have to wait _____ days for the next high tide sufficient to float her off.

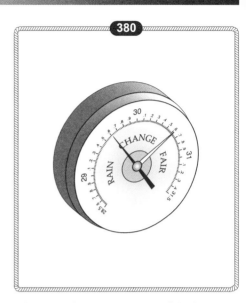

380

A barometric pressure rise or fall of _____ _____ or more per hour indicates bad weather for the sailor.

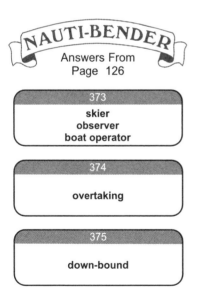

NAUTI-BENDER
Answers From Page 126

373
skier
observer
boat operator

374
overtaking

375
down-bound

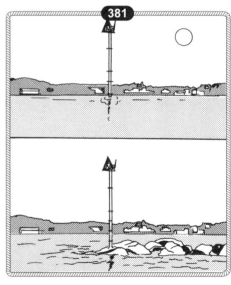

381

The period of little or no water movement between high- and low-tide is referred to as "_____" water.

Red skies during evening hours indicate a
_____ forecast.

A "neap" tide has **higher** or **lower** highs or
higher or **lower** lows.

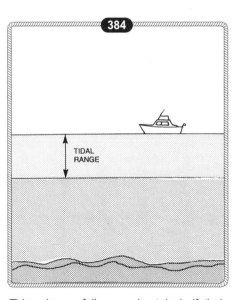

Tides rise or fall approximately half their
range during the **first**, **middle**, or **last** two
hours of the cycle?

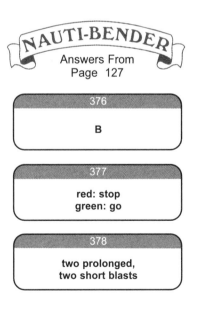

NAUTI-BENDER
Answers From
Page 127

376
B

377
red: stop green: go

378
two prolonged, two short blasts

385

When grounded, protect the topsides from being badly _____ and possibly _____ by placing fenders, cushions, etc. between the hull and bottom.

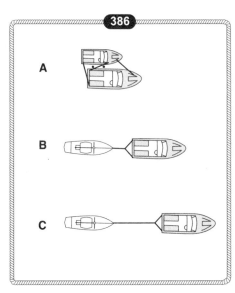

386

A

B

C

There are three basic towing situations (match with the appropriate towing method shown above): ( ) a short tow with no obstructions, ( ) towing with obstructions in calm water, and ( ) towing at sea.

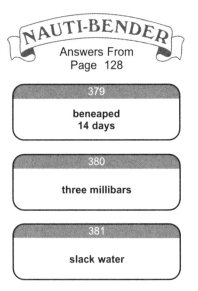

NAUTI-BENDER
Answers From
Page 128

379

beneaped
14 days

380

three millibars

381

slack water

387

When towing at sea or in rough waters, the towline should be as _____ as possible while keeping the two boats in "step". In quiet or protected waters, the towline should be as _____ as possible to allow better handling.

388

You are being towed: Your vessel begins to yaw excessively. What action can you take to reduce the yawing: **shift weight to the stern**, **request a reduction in towing speed**, or **lengthen the tow rope**?

389

Running an inlet with a high, following sea can be dangerous offering the possibility of "_____", "_____", or being "_____" and should be avoided if at all possible.

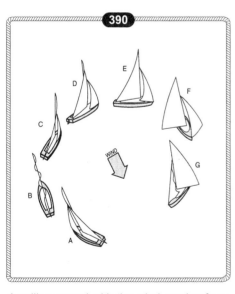

390

A sailing vessel with the wind coming from 219 degrees relative would be: (A) **close-hauled (starboard tack)**, (C) **close-hauled (port tack)**, (D) **broad reach (port tack)**, or (E) **running**.

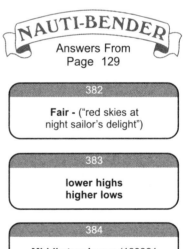

NAUTI-BENDER
Answers From
Page 129

382

Fair - ("red skies at night sailor's delight")

383

lower highs
higher lows

384

Middle two hours (123321 "twelfths" rule-of-thumb)

When sail area is reduced during high winds, it is referred to as "_____".

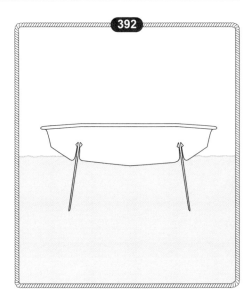

A "_____" is an extremely fast sailboat with two boards that are raised or lowered similar to a centerboard.

Answers From Page 130

385

holed
damaged

386

A: **towing with obstructions**
B: **short tow** (short towline)
C: **Towing at sea** (long towline)

387

long – (rough waters)
short – (quiet waters)

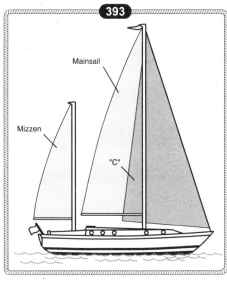

The sail indicated in "**C**" above is referred to as the "_____".

394

The above vessel is referred to as a "_____ _____".

395

Sometimes, when a pleasure boat has been on a long cruise, a greenish stain forms on the bow and is referred to as a "_____".

396

When a vessel flips over, end to end, bow under first, it is referred to as "_____".

NAUTI-BENDER
Answers From
Page 131

388

shift weight to the stern

389

broaching
pitchpoling
pooped

390

broad reach (port tack)

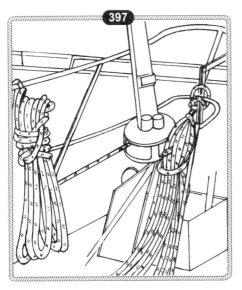

Nylon lines are deteriorated by: **dry rot**, **salt water** or **exposure to the sun**.

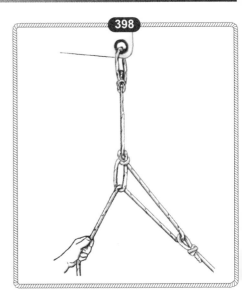

The simple three-part _____ shown above will produce nearly a 3:1 mechanical advantage.

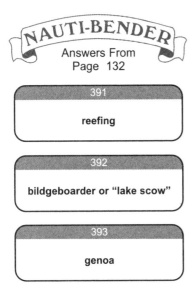

To tie a small line to a larger line so it won't slip, one would use a "_____ _____".

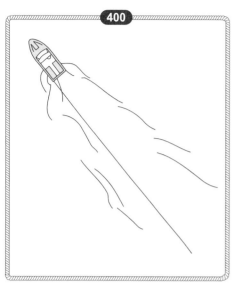

Sometimes anchor rope becomes a mass of kinks when used or stored. The kinks can easily be _____ by dragging the rope astern of a moving boat.

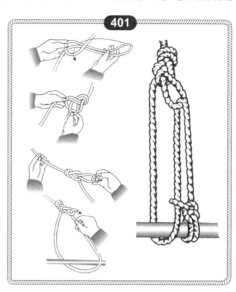

The "_____ _____" is a handy knot for securing a load, such as a dinghy on the foredeck or a small boat on top of the car.

A "bowline" is used to form a temporary _____ at the end of a line.

NAUTI-BENDER
Answers From Page 133

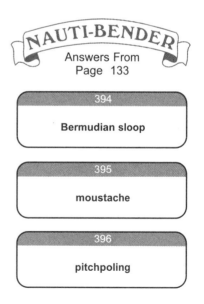

394
Bermudian sloop

395
moustache

396
pitchpoling

"Locking" Technique: for more control and easy departure, "_____" bow and stern lines should be utilized and these lines should always be tended, not cleated (especially on the way down).

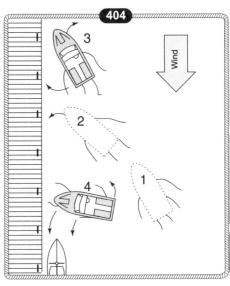

When docking, you're caught in a sudden gust of wind **(position 2)** from ahead: what corrective action is required to avoid getting set down **(position 4)**?

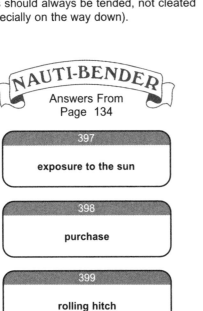

NAUTI-BENDER
Answers From
Page 134

397

exposure to the sun

398

purchase

399

rolling hitch

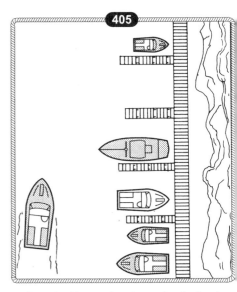

Before docking or leaving a berth the two most important factors to consider are _____ and _____.

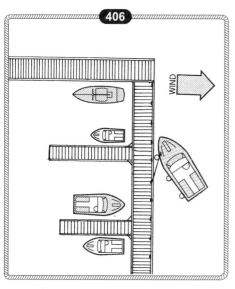

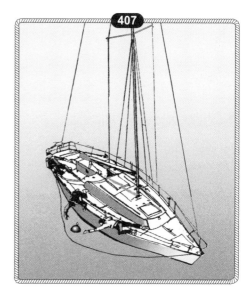

Docking port-side-to with a warp led aft from the center cleat and the engine(s) ahead, hard-right rudder should bring the boat _____ .

Tying up to a buoy without a pennant can be easily accomplished using a **non-buoyant** line in a "_____"; once over, secure both ends to the bow.

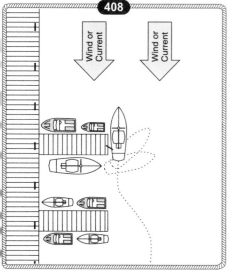

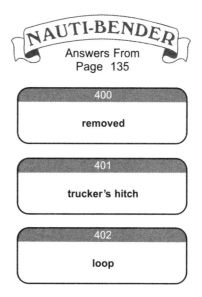

When docking in a strong wind, tide, current, or tight quarters, let the dock lines do the _____ to minimize stress/embarrassing situations for captain and crew.

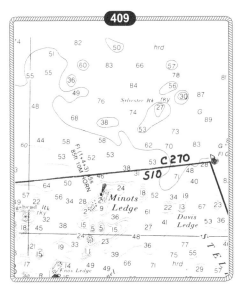

A straight line used in laying out a course on a Mercator chart is referred to as the " _____ _____ ".

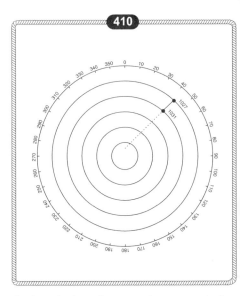

Radar plotting: for any given speed, the distance in yards travelled in three minutes is 100 times the speed; e.g., a vessel making _____ knots will cover 1000 yards in three minutes.

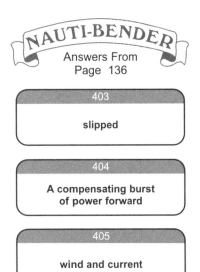

NAUTI-BENDER
Answers From Page 136

403

slipped

404

A compensating burst of power forward

405

wind and current

" _____ _____ _____ " are white lights only. The groups have different combination of flashes; e.g., (1 + 3) or two long and two short flashes.

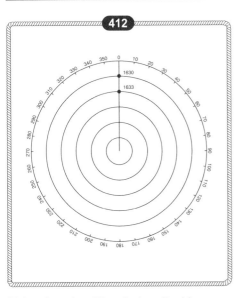

Using the rule of thumb described in question **#410**; assume you are cruising at nine knots, a radar target dead ahead moves 900 yards in three minutes – what is the contact's speed?

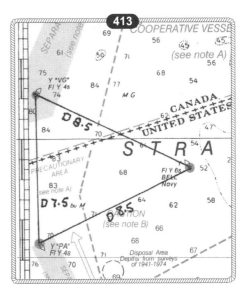

Departing at 0800 hours, what speed is required to complete the course (**Y "PA" to "Y" to Y "VG" and then return to Y "PA"**) by 1200 hours (use dead reckoning formula 60D = ST)?

" _____ _____ _____ " lights have a fixed light broken at regular intervals by a brighter light.

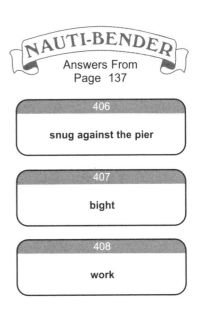

415

In the rare event you should ever have to be rescued by a Coast Guard helicopter, **remember to let the basket hit the water before grabbing it**. The _____ _____ charge could be fatal.

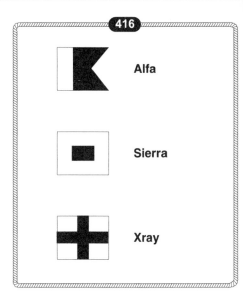

416

Alfa

Sierra

Xray

The international code flags shown above indicate – Alfa: _____ _____ _____ _____; Sierra: _____ _____ _____; Xray: _____ _____ _____.

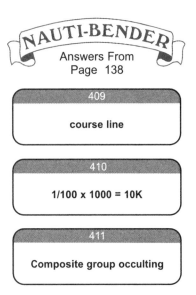

417

What is the distance to the horizon for a mariner with a "height-of-eye" of 9 ft. (i.e., 9 ft. above the water's surface)?

When turning a boat, the compass card or needle **does** or **does not** turn accordingly to indicate direction travelled.

You are offshore when a small plane circles overhead three times gunning its engine, indicating: (A) **you're headed into shoal waters**, (B) **a pod of whales is approaching**, (C) **you should stop**, or (D) **you should follow**.

When completing a radio transmission the proper sign off is "**over**", "**over and out**", or "**out**"?

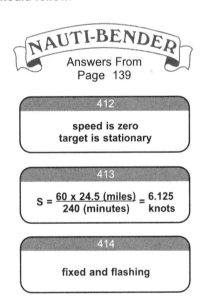

NAUTI-BENDER
Answers From
Page 139

412
speed is zero
target is stationary

413
$S = \frac{60 \times 24.5 \text{ (miles)}}{240 \text{ (minutes)}} = \frac{6.125}{\text{knots}}$

414
fixed and flashing

An amateur yachtsman is sometimes referred to as a "_____".

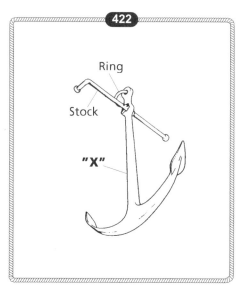

Anchor Nomenclature: "**X**" shown above would be referred to as the "_____".

NAUTI-BENDER
Answers From
Page 140

415

static electric

416

A: Diver down keep clear
S: Engines going astern
X: Stop your intention

417

Formula: $1.14 \times \sqrt{HE}$...

$1.14 \times \sqrt{9} = 3.42$ miles

When a sailboat loses headway when attempting to "come about" it is said to be "_____ _____".

When you "_____" a line, it should be "surged" while maintaining a strain, without parting.

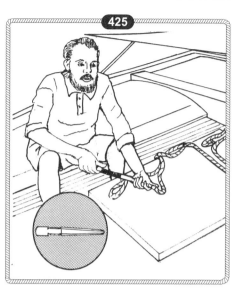

A "_____" is a smooth, tapered tool used for opening stranded line for splicing.

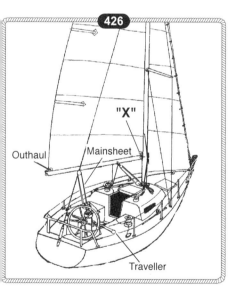

Sail Language: "**X**" shown above would be referred to as the "_____" and is the control line system near the tack of the sail used to adjust luff tension.

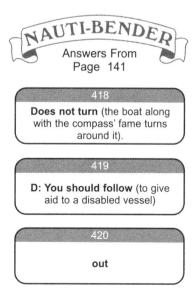

NAUTI-BENDER

Answers From
Page 141

418

Does not turn (the boat along with the compass' fame turns around it).

419

D: You should follow (to give aid to a disabled vessel)

420

out

A braided towline is more preferable over three-strand nylon because: braided is stronger (same diameter), does not kink, and is elastic, but not so much as to create a _____ hazard.

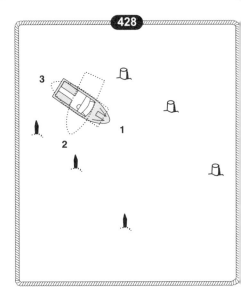

To best turn a twin-screw vessel to the right and about in a narrow channel use: **both engines ahead, ahead right rudder**; **port engine ahead only**; **port engine ahead, starboard astern**; or **both engines astern, right rudder**.

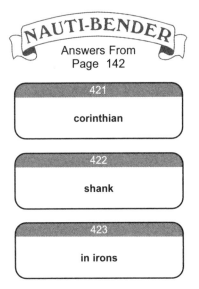

NAUTI-BENDER
Answers From
Page 142

421
corinthian

422
shank

423
in irons

The best tide conditions for crossing a rough bar would be _____-_____ _____.

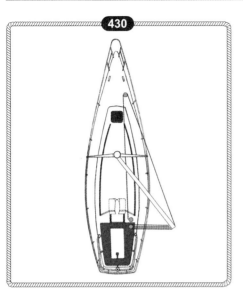

430

To prevent an accidental jibe while sailing down wind: rig a "_____ _____".

431

In thick fog, especially in congested shipping lanes, a dinghy should be towed behind the boat for _____ _____ in an emergency situation.

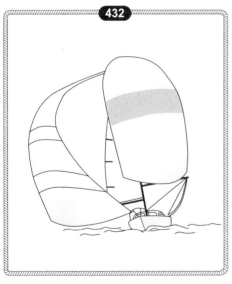

432

Keeping a deep pocket in a sail improves performance in **light** or **heavy** air, particularly while running or reaching.

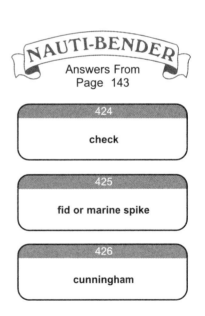

NAUTI-BENDER

Answers From
Page 143

424
check

425
fid or marine spike

426
cunningham

The two most important steps before getting under way, under power (vessels with gasoline engine(s) or propane cooking fuel) are to _____ the bilges and engine compartment for fumes and to run engine blower for at least five minutes.

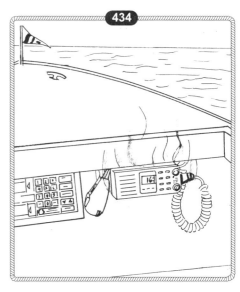

Electrical fires should be extinguished by: first _____ power to the affected unit; then dousing with **water, Type B, Type C,** or **Type BC extinguisher.**

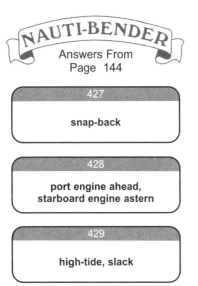

NAUTI-BENDER
Answers From
Page 144

427
snap-back

428
port engine ahead, starboard engine astern

429
high-tide, slack

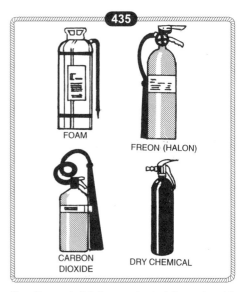

FOAM

FREON (HALON)

CARBON DIOXIDE

DRY CHEMICAL

Small wood, fabric, or alcohol fires should be extinguished by: **dousing with water, Type B** or **Type C extinguisher**.

If a fire breaks out on the stern of your vessel, you should maneuver your bow **into** or **with** the wind?

Rule-of-thumb: "the best time to fight an onboard fire is when it _____ _____ or is a small fire": **Install smoke detectors, fire extinguishers and be familiar with fire fighting procedures.**

Emergency Distress Signal: if flares are inoperative, used up, or not available, try pointing a camera and activating the _____ to attract attention.

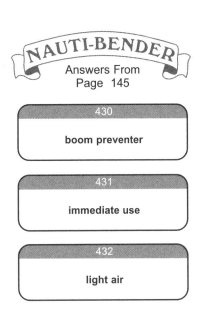

NAUTI-BENDER
Answers From
Page 145

430
boom preventer

431
immediate use

432
light air

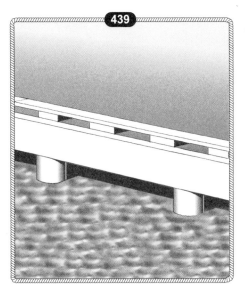

Frequently used short-term docks (public landing, gas docks, etc.) sometimes utilize a "rail" system to facilitate tying-up _____ _____ boats.

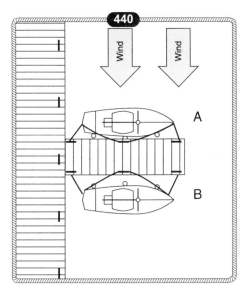

Which slip, "**A**" or "**B**" shown above, would be less strain on the boat and more comfortable for crew in strong wind conditions?

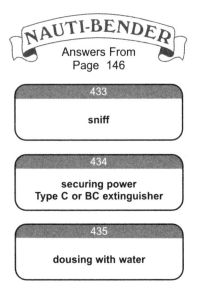

NAUTI-BENDER
Answers From
Page 146

433

sniff

434

securing power
Type C or BC extinguisher

435

dousing with water

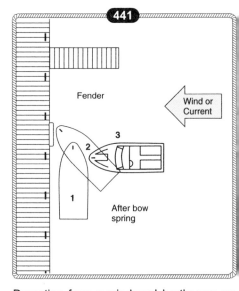

Departing from a windward berth: use an after bow spring, go _____ easy with hard _____ rudder (don't forget fendering).

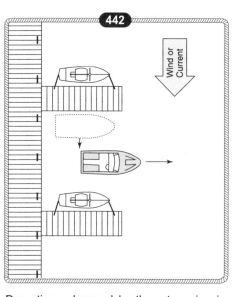

Departing a leeward berth; put engine in _____, cast off all lines (bow and stern last), and when Mother Nature has helped the boat drift clear – motor out.

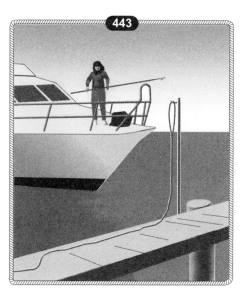

Docking at your regular berth can be made easier by rigging a permanent _____ _____ (correct length with large eye), as shown above.

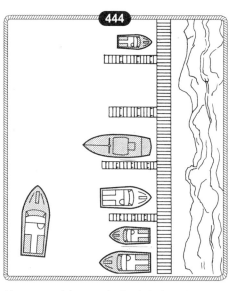

Your vessel has a single right-handed propeller. If you were docking bow-in... would be easier **port** or **starboard** side-to?

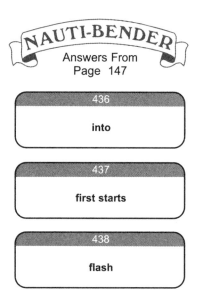

NAUTI-BENDER
Answers From
Page 147

436

into

437

first starts

438

flash

445

To make fenders look like new and avoid time-consuming scrubbing, simply wipe them down with a soft rag and _____.

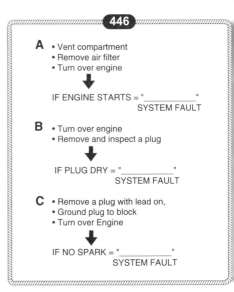

446

A • Vent compartment
• Remove air filter
• Turn over engine

⬇

IF ENGINE STARTS = "_____"
SYSTEM FAULT

B • Turn over engine
• Remove and inspect a plug

⬇

IF PLUG DRY = "_____"
SYSTEM FAULT

C • Remove a plug with lead on,
• Ground plug to block
• Turn over Engine

⬇

IF NO SPARK = "_____"
SYSTEM FAULT

If a gasoline engine fails to start, three basic systems: "**A**" _____, "**B**" _____, and "**C**" _____; should be checked (as described above) until the problem is isolated.

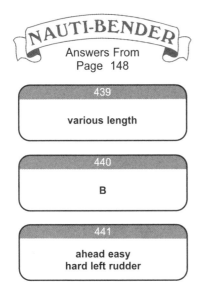

NAUTI-BENDER
Answers From
Page 148

439

various length

440

B

441

**ahead easy
hard left rudder**

447

When changing filters, to prevent your engine(s) from becoming _____ _____ and to protect against unnecessary wear, fill the filters with fuel or lube oil prior to installation.

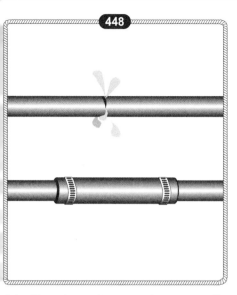

A leaking pipe or hose can be temporarily repaired by placing a _____ diameter section of hose over the leak and securing both ends with hose clamps.

_____ is the main reason why halyards and sheets "part", usually caused by unfair leads.

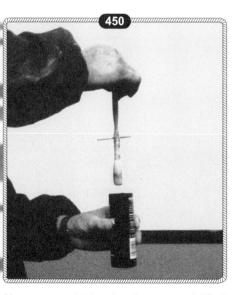

Have your paint brushes become solidified or the bristles stuck together? Before discarding, try dipping the brush in hot _____ for a few minutes then rinsing in soapy water.

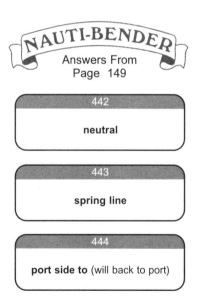

NAUTI-BENDER
Answers From
Page 149

442
neutral

443
spring line

444
port side to (will back to port)

451

The above illustrates one method to _____ a helpless person who has fallen overboard.

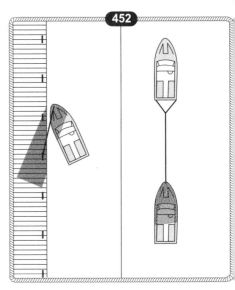

452

The _____ of nylon line under load creates danger zones which should be avoided.

453

The effective range of a 15 lb. CO_2 extinguisher is: **2 to 4 feet**, **3 to 8 feet**, or **9 to 12 feet**.

How long are distress flares approved for – **30-, 42-, or 60-months** from the date of manufacture?

When discharging a CO_2 fire extinguisher, the horn should not be held because it will become extremely **hot** or **cold**.

_____ is the major single cause of small boat accidents.

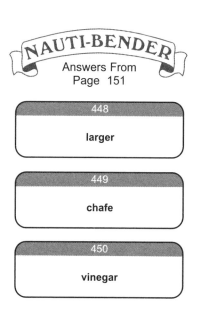

NAUTI-BENDER

Answers From
Page 151

448
larger

449
chafe

450
vinegar

When in doubt or in danger a vessel should sound _____ or more short blasts.

A "prolonged" blast is typically _____ second(s) in length.

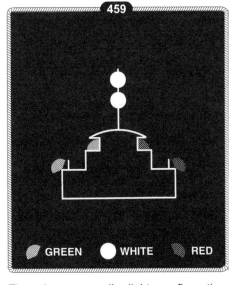

GREEN ● WHITE RED

The above vessel's light configuration would indicate she is _____ _____.

Using a high-intensity strobe light to attract attention on the high seas is an accepted practice – **true** or **false**?

While cruising in fog, you hear a signal ahead (a long blast followed by two short blasts) indicating a vessel is engaged in: **fishing**, **towing or pushing**, **sailing** or **all of the above**.

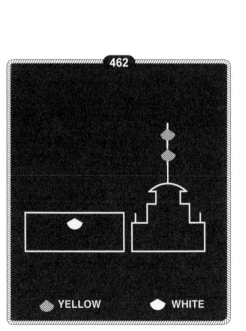

The above vessel's light configuration would indicate she is _____.

YELLOW   WHITE

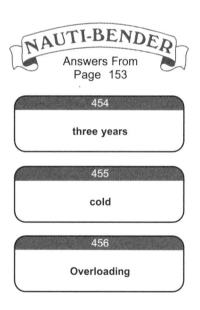

NAUTI-BENDER

Answers From
Page 153

454
three years

455
cold

456
Overloading

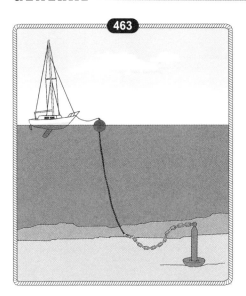

Minimum space between moorings should be _____ times total scope plus the boat's length.

464

1. Description of Boat:
   • Type _____ • Color_____
   • Reg. # _____ • Length _____
   • Name _____ • Make _____

2. Persons Aboard _____

3. Any Medical Problems _____

4. Trip Expectations
   • Leave at_____
   • From _____
   • Going to _____
   • Return By_____

5. If not returned by _____ call Coast Guard
   (xxx) xxx-xxxx.

Before getting under way your checklist should include **fuel, lubrication and bilge levels**; **weather forecast**; and/or **leaving a float plan**.

NAUTI-BENDER
Answers From
Page 154

457

5 or more short blasts

458

four to six seconds

459

towing astern (tow less than 200M)

The distance to a thunderstorm can be determined by counting the seconds (1001, 1002, etc.) between the lightning flash and thunder clap. Each second equals approximately _____.

466

THE PHONETIC ALPHABET

A-Alpha	J-Juliet	S-Sierra
B-Bravo	K-Kilo	T-Tango
C-Charlie	**L-**	U-Uniform
D-	M-Mike	V-Victor
E-Echo	N-November	W-Whiskey
F-Foxtrot	O-Oscar	X-Xray
G-Golf	P-Papa	Y-Yankee
H-Hotel	Q-Quebec	Z-Zulu
I-India	**R-**	

The phonetic or military alphabet words are typically used in shipboard VHF radio communications for clarity. The phonetic words for **D**, **R**, **L** are _____ _____ _____?

467

Generally speaking, the **longer** or **shorter** the VHF antenna, the greater its gain or effective range.

468

Engine/steering controls on smaller boats are typically installed on the _____ side, providing the operator better visibility of his/her "_____ _____".

NAUTI-BENDER
Answers From
Page 155

460
false (a strobe light is only used as an official distress signal on inland waters)

461
all of the above

462
towing alongside

469

One method to "refloat" your boat after running aground is to set a "_____" anchor and "_____" her over to reduce her draft.

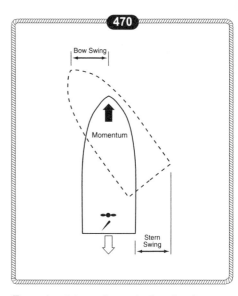

470

Every boat turns by swinging the **bow** or **stern**.

471

A vessel carrying sails with a high "aspect ratio" will perform better **close-hauled**, **broad-reaching** or **running**?

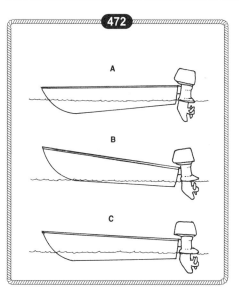

A boat in proper _____ achieves better fuel economy and speed. Which of the boats shown above is in proper _____?

While backing on twin-engines (rudder amidships) your port engine stalls. To continue backing in a straight line: **apply left rudder**, **apply right rudder**, or **apply a burst of power on the starboard engine**.

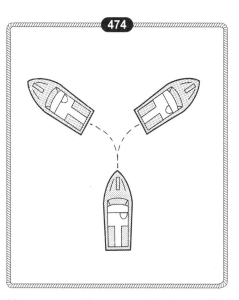

You are operating a powerboat on a fair sea. A passenger falls overboard on the port side. You should take a hard turn to the **port** or **starboard**?

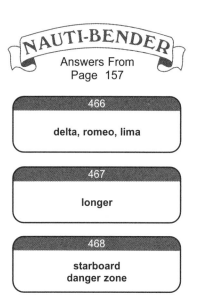

NAUTI-BENDER
Answers From Page 157

466

delta, romeo, lima

467

longer

468

starboard
danger zone

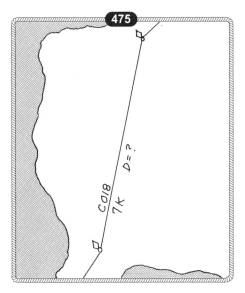

70 nautical miles would be equal to roughly _____ statute miles.

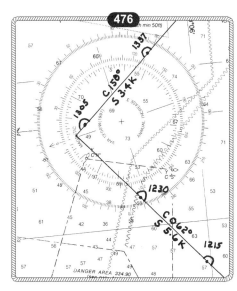

Dead reckoning or "DR" positions are determined by calculating the vessel's position using courses steered, time elapsed, and speed made. The term "dead" evolves from "ded", the abbreviated form of _____.

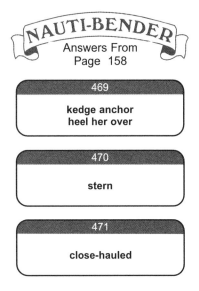

NAUTI-BENDER
Answers From
Page 158

469

**kedge anchor
heel her over**

470

stern

471

close-hauled

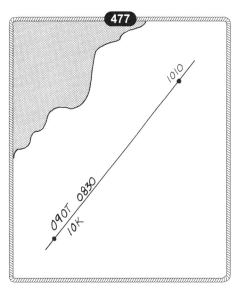

How far would you travel in an hour and 40 minutes if you were making at 10 knots?

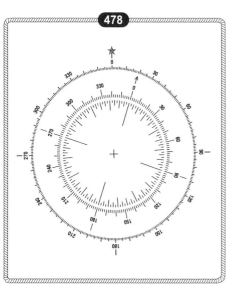

Variation is not constant; it increases or decreases by the amount shown in the center of the "_____ _____" on an _____ basis.

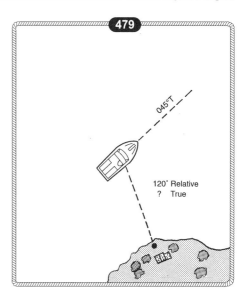

If your vessel was heading 025° true and a lighthouse was spotted at 120° relative: what would be the true bearing to the lighthouse?

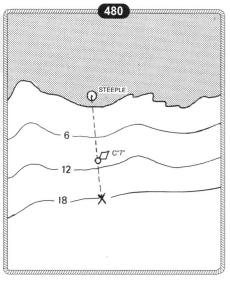

Coming abeam of a can, with a depth reading of 18 ft... could you assume that you were approximately at point "**X**" (above)?

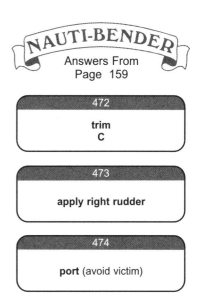

481

"_____" is a term originating from accommodations on early British merchantmen offering cabins on the port side going out and the starboard side coming home for wealthy passengers to avoid the sun's heat and glare.

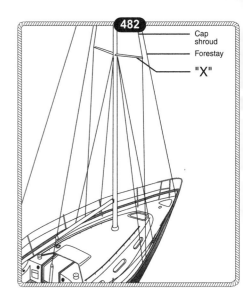

482

Cap shroud
Forestay
"X"

Sail Language: "**X**", shown above, would be referred to as the _____.

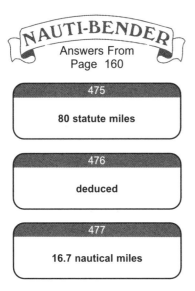

NAUTI-BENDER
Answers From
Page 160

475
80 statute miles

476
deduced

477
16.7 nautical miles

483

A sailboat with an especially large engine(s) which is not extremely efficient in either mode of propulsion is called a "_____ _____".

When a skipper is very familiar with certain waters, he is said to have "_____ _____".

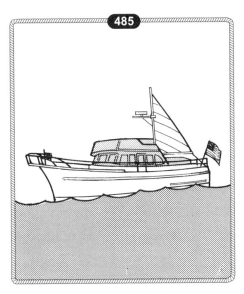

Trawler type boats typically incorporate a small "_____" sail to dampen the effect of the seas.

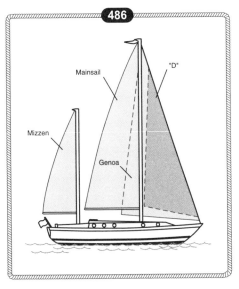

Mainsail

"D"

Mizzen

Genoa

The sail indicated in "**D**" above is referred to as the "_____ _____".

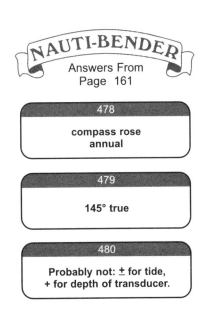

NAUTI-BENDER
Answers From Page 161

478

compass rose
annual

479

145° true

480

Probably not: ± for tide,
+ for depth of transducer.

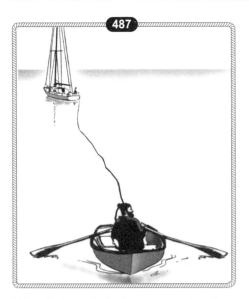

When laying out a kedge or second anchor, it is easier to row if the anchor rode is payed out from the **dinghy** or the **boat**?

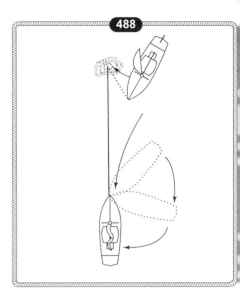

When anchoring under sail in _____ _____, you may want to drop the hook on a run to dig it in quickly without losing steerageway.

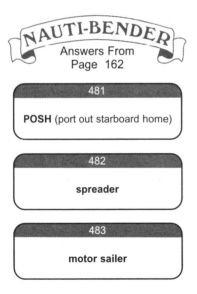

NAUTI-BENDER
Answers From
Page 162

481

POSH (port out starboard home)

482

spreader

483

motor sailer

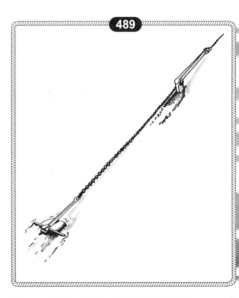

Expecting a blow, anchors laid in "_____" can be quite effective. The adjoining chain should be taut (for maximum holding) and be 1½ times the water's depth for easy retrieval.

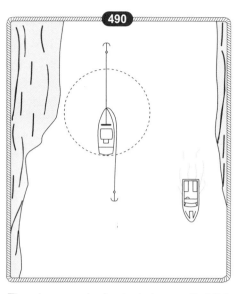

The above anchoring technique called the "_____ _____", is useful to reduce swing circle in tight anchorages.

A "_____ _____" can be rigged for small to relatively large boats, and are great in rough anchorages or where there is limited dockage (hint: keep line well spread apart to avoid tangles).

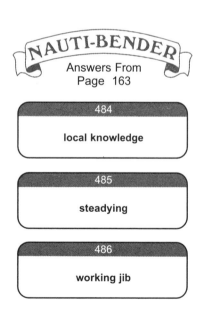

NAUTI-BENDER

Answers From
Page 163

484
local knowledge

485
steadying

486
working jib

A "haul-off" can be rigged as shown above to compensate for tide and protect your boat from wake-damage at busy-harbor dockages. Typically, a _____ pound weight will hold off a 4500-pound boat.

493

Cruising southward along the California coast, you encounter a buoy with a flashing red light: the buoy should be passed on the **starboard side**, **port side**, or **either side well clear**.

494

The vessel above is displaying a day shape indicating she is _____.

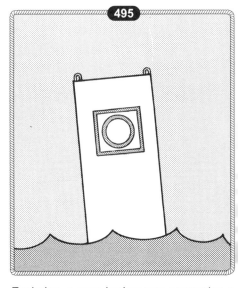

495

Exploring a new harbor you encounter a white buoy with orange stripes. This buoy indicates _____ _____.

Entering from sea, you encounter a red and green horizontally-banded buoy. The top band is green, indicating the preferred channel is with the buoy to the **port** or **starboard** of your boat.

A buoy or marker's shape always indicates its color – **true** or **false**?

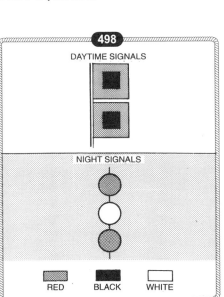

The above signal indicates a "_____" weather warning with winds above_____ knots.

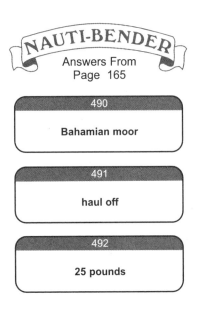

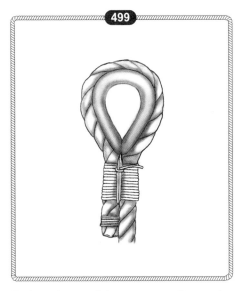

499

Rather than splicing an eye, it can be lashed with seizing. This method is especially useful with _____ or _____ rope.

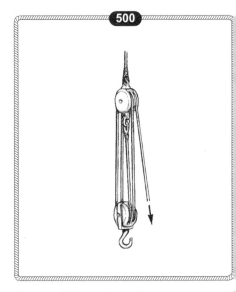

500

The two-fold purchase shown above would produce a mechanical advantage of **X4** or **X5**?

501

Lashing mooring pennants at regular intervals with "_____ _____" will avoid tangles and strength-diminishing kinks.

502

The "_____ _____" is probably the best knot used to join two lines together.

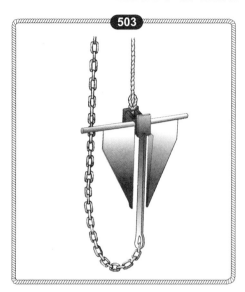

503

Sometimes anchors become fouled in the seabed; the best way to avoid the problem is to rig a _____ line to the anchor (secured to a buoy or onboard).

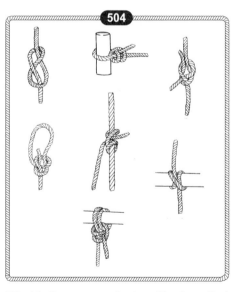

504

What is the common factor with all nautical knots?

505

If it's required to move a boat single-handedly, the above method will keep the _____ pointed out and keep her from rubbing along the _____.

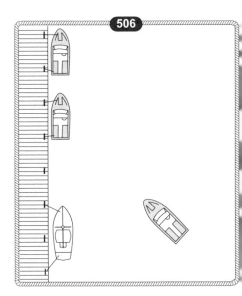

506

The best conditions to maneuver into a tight slip would be: **with the wind off the dock**, **with the wind onto the dock**, **at slack tide**, or **with a cross current**.

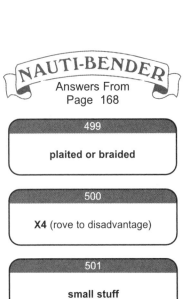

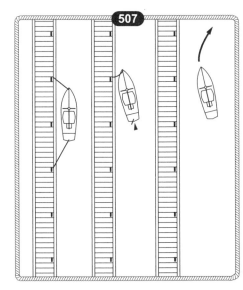

507

The above unberthing procedure would be proper with wind and tide coming from _____.

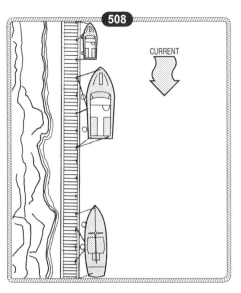

When docking alongside a pier, one should approach **against** or **with** the current for more control.

In very tight quarters even the most experienced captain may have to use the "hand-over-hand" maneuvering technique and "_____" the boat in.

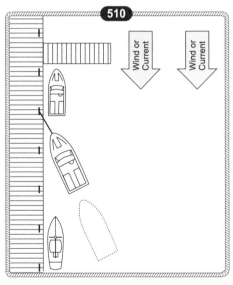

Docking into strong wind or tide: approach the pier at the tightest angle possible, secure the bow line, and let the boat _____ back into position.

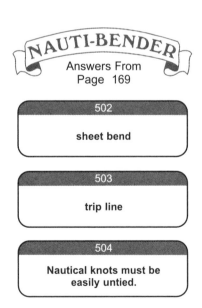

LANGUAGE

The above vessel is referred to as a
"_____".

The "_____" anchor is good for anchoring in _____ but not the best choice for all-around use.

NAUTI-BENDER
Answers From
Page 170

505

bow
pier

506

at slack tide

507

behind

The above vessel used 10 fathoms of anchor rode or _____ feet.

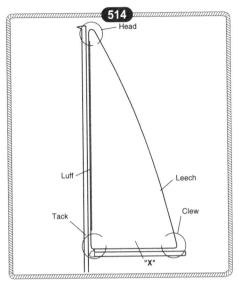

Sail Language: "**X**" shown above would be referred to as the "_____".

The above vessel is referred to as a "_____".

In the Great Lakes a temporary (few minutes to several hours) rise or fall of water may occur and is referred to as "_____". This fluctuation is typically caused by sudden changes in barometric pressure or strong winds.

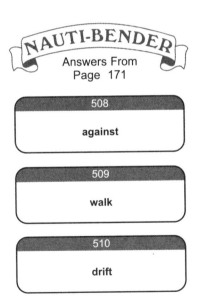

NAUTI-BENDER
Answers From
Page 171

508
against

509
walk

510
drift

BOAT HANDLING

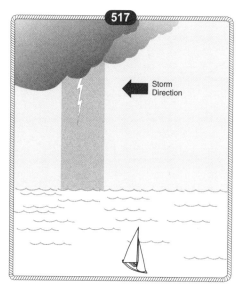

Sailing well away from an isolated thunderstorm, the wind will be _____.

Which vessel is "jibbing"?

NAUTI-BENDER
Answers From Page 172

511

ketch

512

yachtsman
rocks

513

60 feet

In an imminent collision situation (assuming converging courses), turning to **port** or **starboard** will increase your (sailboat) chances of avoidance.

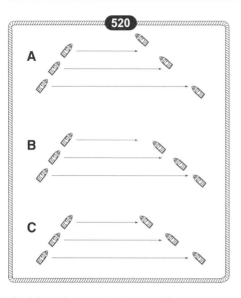

Cruising at a constant speed/course, you observe a vessel at 2 o'clock. What do the sighted bearings ("**A**", "**B**", "**C**" above) taken off the same fixed object on your vessel indicate?

The best way to handle heavy weather is to _____ _____.

The "_____ _____" is set above the standard jib and is usually "_____" to the forestay.

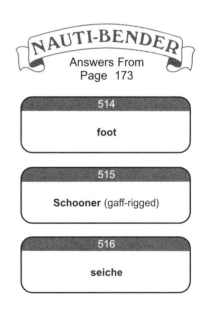

NAUTI-BENDER
Answers From
Page 173

514
foot

515
Schooner (gaff-rigged)

516
seiche

When approaching a fog bank, the boat's speed must be reduced so it can stop within, **25%**, **50%** or **100%** of the visibility distance.

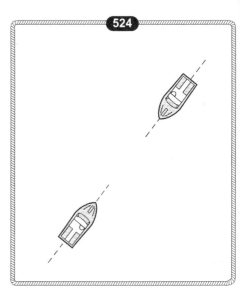

Meeting a vessel head-on you should pass _____ to _____.

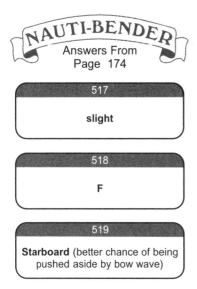

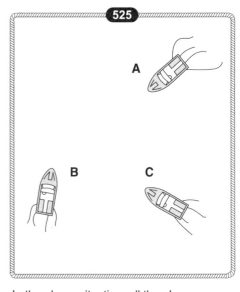

In the above situation, all the pleasure vessels are moving forward. Which vessel has the right of way or is the stand-on vessel?

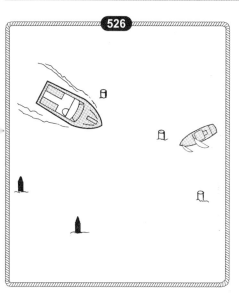

A vessel crossing a river, channel, or fairway must give way to any vessel ascending or descending – **true** or **false**?

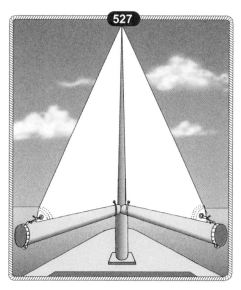

Right-of-way rule-of-thumb: when two vessels that are sailing meet head-to-head, if your boom is on starboard – _____ _____; if on port – _____.

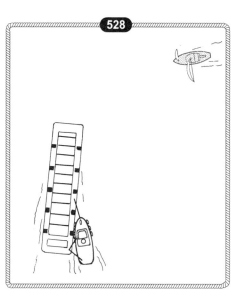

Sailing in Boston Harbor you note you are on a rapidly closing collision course with a tug pushing a barge ahead... **who has the right-of-way**?

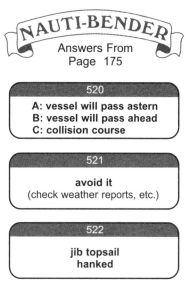

NAUTI-BENDER
Answers From
Page 175

520
A: vessel will pass astern
B: vessel will pass ahead
C: collision course

521
avoid it
(check weather reports, etc.)

522
jib topsail
hanked

Typically, how does a **whisker pole** differ from a **spinnaker pole**?

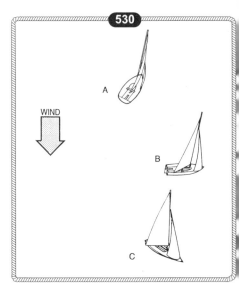

Apparent wind would have the greatest effect on which vessel shown above?

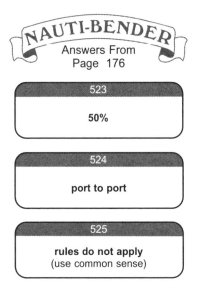

NAUTI-BENDER
Answers From
Page 176

523
50%

524
port to port

525
rules do not apply (use common sense)

Which two of the Great Lakes are considered hydraulically as one: **Superior/Huron**, **Michigan/Huron**, or **Erie/Ontario?**

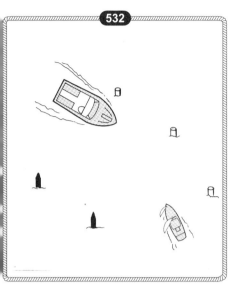

532

A sailboat **does** or **does not** have to keep clear of a powerboat that cannot navigate outside the channel it's using.

533

Using obscene, indecent, or profane language during radio communication is punishable by a _____ fine, imprisonment for _____ years, or both.

534

A boat engine's average life expectancy is – gasoline: _____ hours and diesel: _____ hours depending on use and maintenance performed.

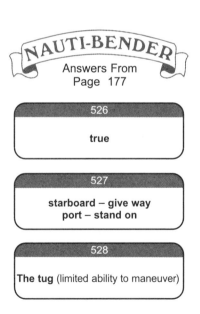

NAUTI-BENDER
Answers From
Page 177

526

true

527

starboard – give way
port – stand on

528

The tug (limited ability to maneuver)

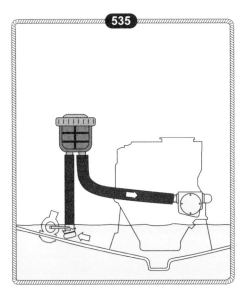

In a "sinking" situation a boat's engine can be "jury rigged" into an additional _____ system.

A fire erupts in your engine. What should the skipper do first?

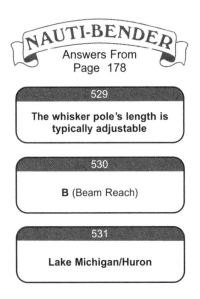

Typical marine fire extinguishers have a discharge time of... **30- to 60-seconds**, **1- to 2-minutes**, or **8- to 20-seconds**?

Typically, it is a **lack** or **lapse** of _____ that gets boaters in trouble while on-the-water.

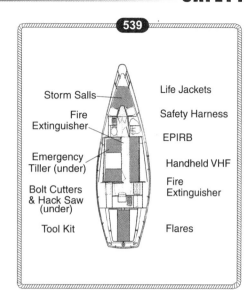

Storm Sails
Fire Extinguisher
Emergency Tiller (under)
Bolt Cutters & Hack Saw (under)
Tool Kit

Life Jackets
Safety Harness
EPIRB
Handheld VHF
Fire Extinguisher
Flares

It is good practice to generate an _____ _____ _____ that is prominently displayed for crew and passengers in the event the captain should fall overboard or otherwise become disabled.

A fire extinguisher is most effective when aimed at the... **top of the flames**; **base of the fire**; or **at the smoke**.

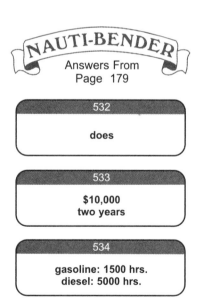

NAUTI-BENDER
Answers From
Page 179

532
does

533
$10,000 **two years**

534
gasoline: 1500 hrs. **diesel: 5000 hrs.**

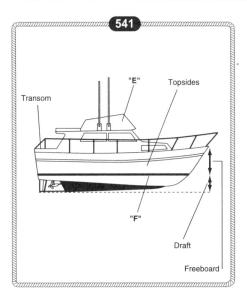

541

Hull Language: "**E**" and "**F**" (shown above) would be referred to as the _____ and _____.

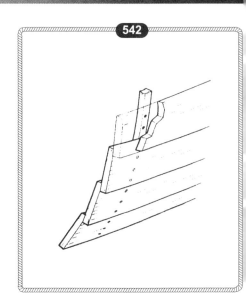

542

"_____" construction: a method of boat building in which the lower edge of each side plank overlaps the upper edge of the one below it.

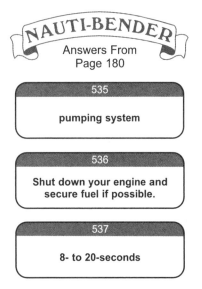

NAUTI-BENDER
Answers From
Page 180

535

pumping system

536

Shut down your engine and secure fuel if possible.

537

8- to 20-seconds

543

When a vessel is kept meticulous in every detail it is said to be kept in "_____ _____".

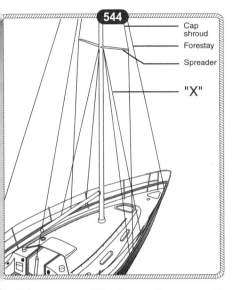

Cap
shroud
Forestay
Spreader

"X"

Sail Language: "**X**", shown above, would be referred to as the _____ _____ _____.

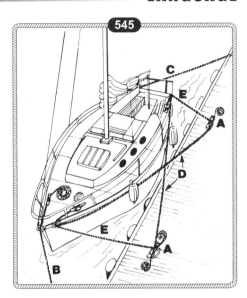

The boat is prevented from sawing back and forth by the "spring" lines "_____" shown above.

The **harbor pilot**, **radio speaker**, **lower steering station**, or **auto pilot** is sometimes referred to as "Iron Mike".

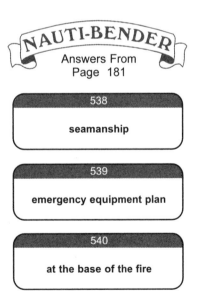

NAUTI-BENDER
Answers From
Page 181

538
seamanship

539
emergency equipment plan

540
at the base of the fire

547

"_____ _____" lights are white and consist of groups of two or more occulting lights (lights that are illuminated more than they're dark).

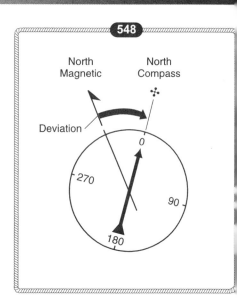

548

North Magnetic

North Compass

Deviation

0

270

90

180

If cruising in an area where the variation is East, the compass course will be _____ than the true course.

NAUTI-BENDER
Answers From Page 182

541

E: Fly Bridge
F: Waterline (length)

542

Lapstrake (in U.S.A.)
Clinker (in Europe)

543

bristol fashion

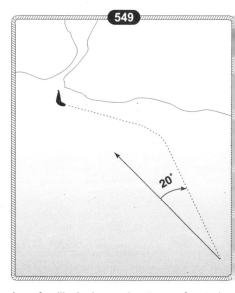

549

20°

In unfamiliar/unbuoyed waters or fog, trying to navigate directly (without Loran-C or GPS) to a river, harbor entrance, etc. is tricky. To eliminate confusion overshoot the _____ course and then follow shore line.

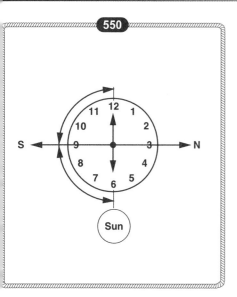

Approximate direction can be determined by a perpendicular line midway between the hour hand and 12 o'clock indicating south in the _____ hemisphere and north in the _____ hemisphere.

"_____" lights show a single flash at regular intervals, with the period of light always being shorter than the period of darkness.

If you're in thick fog and wish to determine the approximate distance to shore, blow your air horn (aimed towards land) and count the seconds for the echo to return. Ten seconds would equal approximately _____ mile(s).

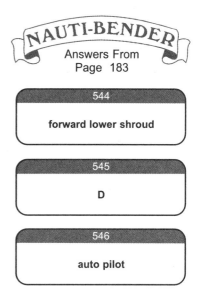

NAUTI-BENDER

Answers From
Page 183

544
forward lower shroud

545
D

546
auto pilot

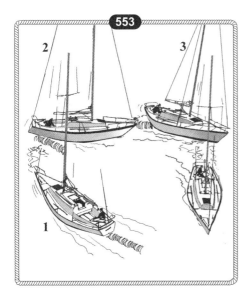

To turn in a tight circle (inboard, right-handed prop): **1.** apply a burst of power _____, hard _____ rudder; **2.** burst of power _____, hard _____ rudder; **3.** keep her turning with another burst _____.

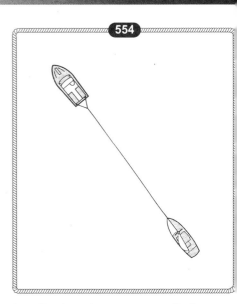

Lengthening a tow rope generally **decreases** or **increases** the maneuverability of the towboat?

When sailing close-hauled (sails trimmed tight), if you ease the sheets, you will sail **faster** or **slower**?

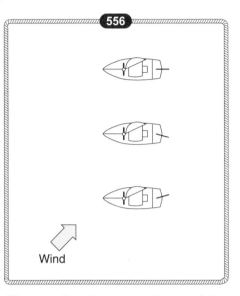

556

557

When a sailboat is in proper "balance", the boat will have **no helm**, **a slight weather** or **lee helm**?

"One-third" fuel rule: one-third out, one-third in, and one-third in _____.

558

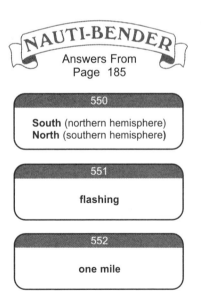

NAUTI-BENDER

Answers From
Page 185

550
South (northern hemisphere) **North** (southern hemisphere)

551
flashing

552
one mile

When underway ahead, increasing speed tends to move the pivot point farther **astern** or **forward**?

559

When tying up to a fixed pier, one must allow for tidal changes. Mooring lines should be at least **three**, **four** or **five** times the rise/fall distance.

560

A twin-screw vessel in a calm or no-wind situation can be "walked" in between two docked boats by setting the rudder _____, the port engine _____ and the starboard engine _____.

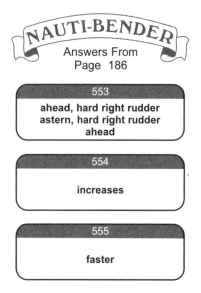

NAUTI-BENDER
Answers From
Page 186

553
ahead, hard right rudder
astern, hard right rudder
ahead

554
increases

555
faster

561

When departing from a mooring (no wind/current) you should: (A) **apply a short burst of power, hard-right rudder**; (B) **back a few boat lengths and proceed normally**; or (C) **go half-ahead, hard-right rudder to clear the buoy**.

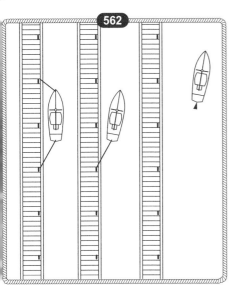

The above unberthing procedure would be proper with the wind coming from _____ _____ _____.

When backing down, a vessel's pivot point is about _____ of the vessel's length from the stern.

When docking with non-crew, shoreside line-handlers pass over the _____ end of the line, thus, keeping "control" (line length, surging, when cleated, etc.).

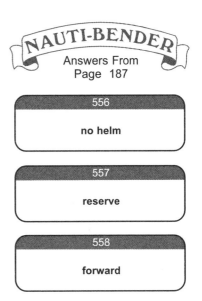

NAUTI-BENDER
Answers From
Page 187

556
no helm

557
reserve

558
forward

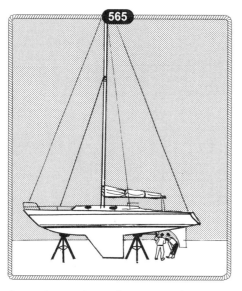

Barnacles can be easily removed from your prop(s) by bathing the prop(s) in _____ acid until the barnacles are dissolved.

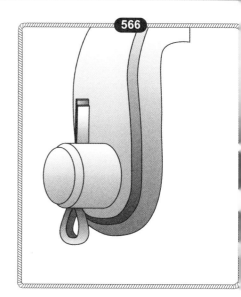

When installing a cotter pin, it should project approximately _____ the fitting's width and spread at an angle of about _____ degrees, then be protected with a couple of wraps of tape.

NAUTI-BENDER
Answers From
Page 188

559

three times

560
rudder hard right,
port engine back,
starboard ahead

561
B: back a few boat lengths
and proceed normally.

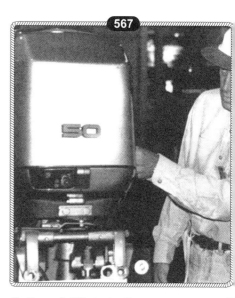

Outboard Winterization: gear case oil should be changed each fall. If water has entered, the oil will look _____; it could freeze and expand, damaging seals or crack the case itself.

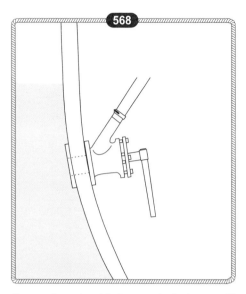

Seacocks should be cycled (opened/closed) on a regular basis to prevent corrosion buildup, and they should be lubricated every _____ months or so.

Smoke from exhaust (gasoline engine): a weak fuel/air mixture or insufficient fuel will produce _____ smoke.

To avoid crushing an oil filter while trying to remove it with a filter wrench, place the wrench at the very _____ or _____ where the filter is the strongest.

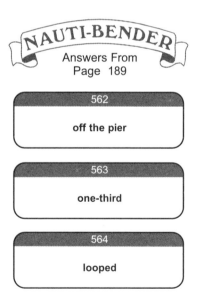

NAUTI-BENDER
Answers From
Page 189

562
off the pier

563
one-third

564
looped

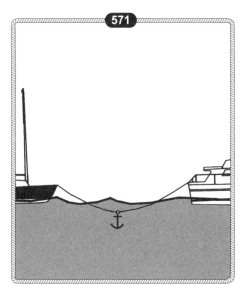

When towing in rough seas, if the tow-line is kept taut, undue stress will be put on both vessels' deck hardware. One method to reduce this stress is to maintain a _____ to keep the tow-line under water at all times.

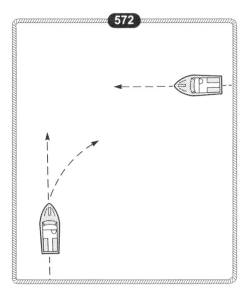

Crossing **ahead** of or **aft** of is typically the best practice to avoid collision.

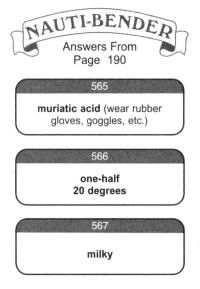

NAUTI-BENDER
Answers From
Page 190

565

muriatic acid (wear rubber gloves, goggles, etc.)

566

**one-half
20 degrees**

567

milky

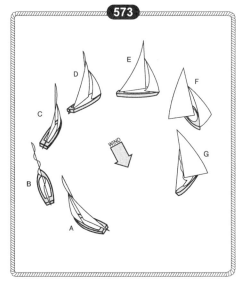

Which vessel is "reaching"?

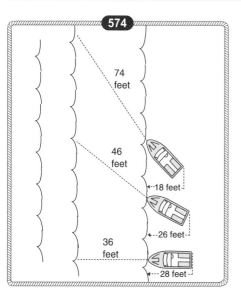

74 feet

46 feet

←18 feet→

←-26 feet-→

36 feet

←-28 feet-→

Instead of heading directly into high seas, try "angling" into them. Depending on the angle, this tactic can increase the "wave to boat length ratio" by up to _____, thus creating a more comfortable ride.

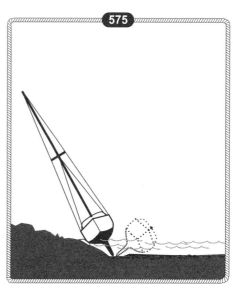

A grounded boat should be "_____" over on the side away from the rising water, otherwise she may be flooded by an incoming tide.

The proper method to maneuver a mooring "pick-up buoy" is **with** or **into the wind**?

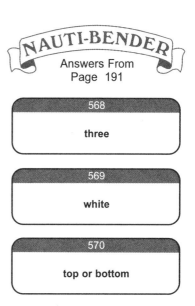

NAUTI-BENDER
Answers From Page 191

568
three

569
white

570
top or bottom

577

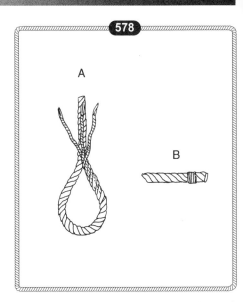
578

The bowline, "king of nautical knots", typically should not be utilized as shown above, because it cannot be undone under _____.

A. When making an eye splice on the end of a line – how many "tucks" are recommended? **B**. The "lay" of a line refers to the _____ of twist in the strands (when held vertically in front of you).

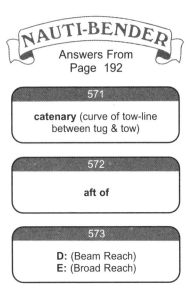

NAUTI-BENDER
Answers From
Page 192

571
catenary (curve of tow-line between tug & tow)

572
aft of

573
D: (Beam Reach)
E: (Broad Reach)

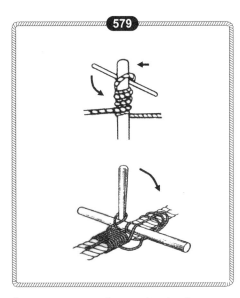
579

" _____ _____ ", a simple leverage method (as shown above) used to draw "seizing" or lashings taut. The same principle can be utilized (like a turnbuckle) in any situation involving rope.

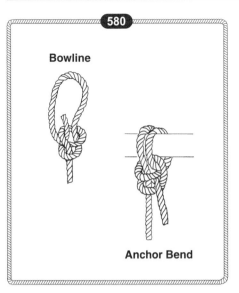

580

Bowline

Anchor Bend

Considering that a line's strength is diminished in varying degrees when tied with different knots, would a **bowline** or **anchor bend** be preferable when rigging a tow-line to a boat's bow eye?

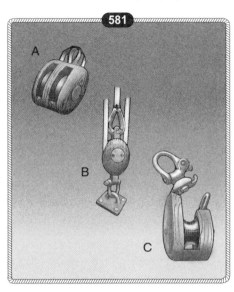

581

A

B

C

Identify the blocks shown above "**A**", "**B**", and "**C**".

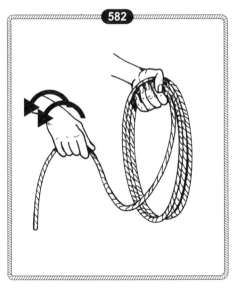

582

To avoid kinks when coiling a line (right-handed lay), twist your wrist a quarter turn _____ with each loop.

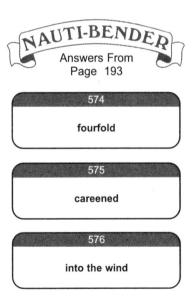

NAUTI-BENDER
Answers From
Page 193

574
fourfold

575
careened

576
into the wind

583

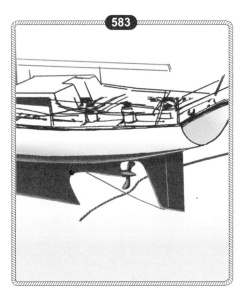

Is your prop protected? Attaching a wire from the _____ to the _____ will help keep out lobster trap lines, sail bags, nets, etc..

584

Identify the organizations the above flags represent; which organization has law enforcement authority?

NAUTI-BENDER
Answers From
Page 194

577

strain

578

A: **four** (However, an extra one for good measure never hurts).
B: **Direction**

579

spanish windlass

585

What is the maximum civil penalty for discharging oil in U.S. waters?

Water-ski hand-signal shown above indicates: _____.

VHF communications – which of the following channels should be utilized for contacting the marine operator: **13**, **16**, **22A**, **24**, **27**, **71** or **72**?

Theoretically, how far will a "15¾ /17" propeller propel the boat forward (inches) with one revolution of the prop?

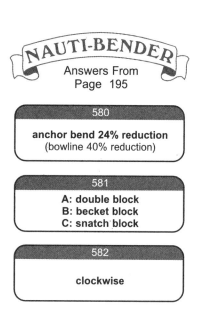

NAUTI-BENDER
Answers From
Page 195

580

anchor bend 24% reduction
(bowline 40% reduction)

581

A: double block
B: becket block
C: snatch block

582

clockwise

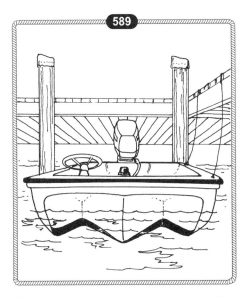

589

The above hull design offers more stability than other hull designs of similar length and is called a "_____ _____ or _____-_____."

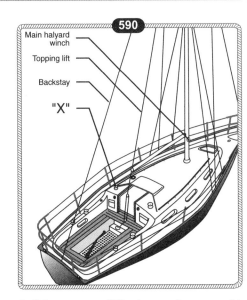

590

Main halyard winch

Topping lift

Backstay

"X"

Sail Language: "X", shown above, would be referred to as the _____ _____ _____.

NAUTI-BENDER
Answers From Page 196

583

skeg to the keel

584

1. **C.G. Aux.** 2. **U.S.C.G.** (has law enforcement authority)
3. **U.S. Power Squadron**

585

Up to a $5,000 fine.

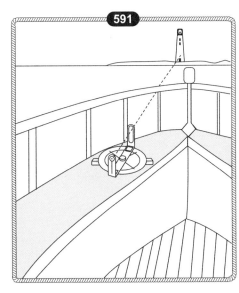

591

A "_____" or "dumb compass" is an instrument with which "_____ _____" are taken.

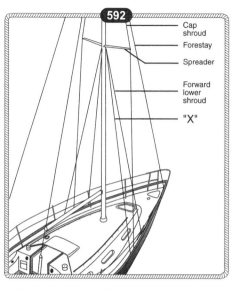

Sail Language: "**X**", shown above, would be referred to as the _____ _____ _____.

A powerful small boat that pushes or pulls an unpowered passenger schooner is called a "_____ _____".

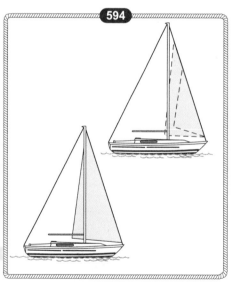

A "jib" is distinguished from a "genoa" by **location**, **size**, or **height**, the genoa being _____.

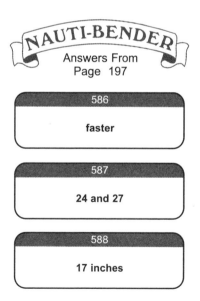

NAUTI-BENDER
Answers From
Page 197

586

faster

587

24 and 27

588

17 inches

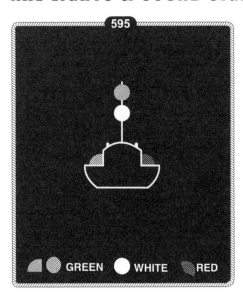

595

GREEN WHITE RED

Navigation Lights: "Green over white, _____ in sight".

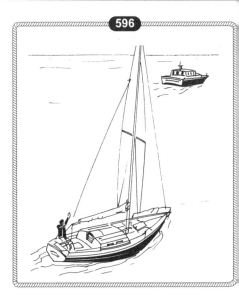

596

A continuous fog signal indicates – a vessel in _____.

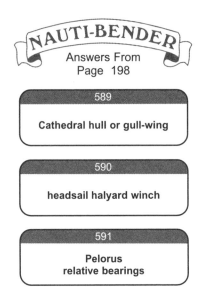
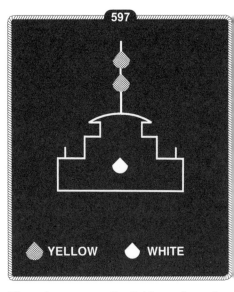

597

YELLOW WHITE

The above vessel's light configuration would indicate she is _____ _____.

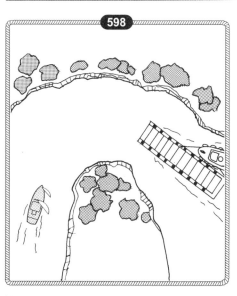

When a vessel is approaching a bend in a river where oncoming traffic cannot be seen, the vessel should sound **one** or **two** prolonged blast(s)?

A vessel less than **5-**, **7-**, or **12-meters** long is not required to show an anchor light **if** anchored in an area not normally navigated.

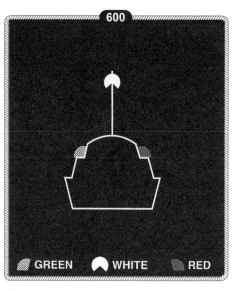

The above vessel's light configuration would indicate she is a _____ _____ underway.

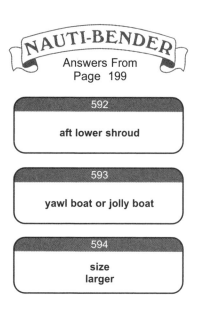

LANGUAGE

601

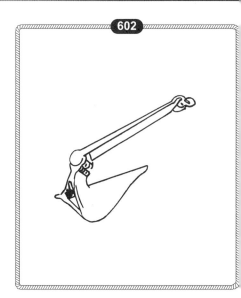

Flag etiquette – in the strictest sense, pleasure vessels that are "documented" are **required** to fly the _____ _____ while in U.S. waters.

602

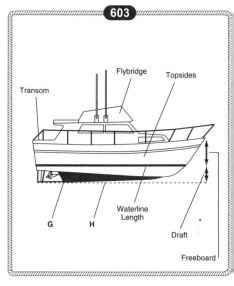

The "_____ or _____" anchor is particularly good for anchoring in _____ or _____.

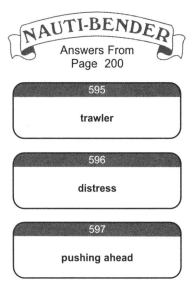

NAUTI-BENDER
Answers From Page 200

595

trawler

596

distress

597

pushing ahead

603

Hull Language: "**G**" and "**H**" shown above would be referred to as the "_____" and "_____ _____".

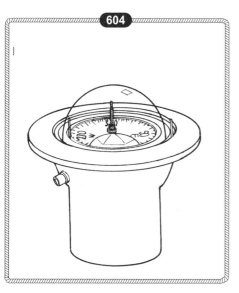

The mark usually inside a compass from which one reads the course or steers is referred to as the "_____ _____".

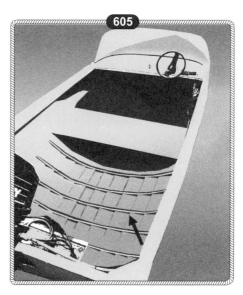

Most boats, regardless of size, have a series of "_____" holes cut or built into their transverse members which allow bilge water to drain to the lowest point.

A most obvious difference between a "yawl" and a "ketch" is the after mast is stepped **before** or **after** the rudder post in a yawl.

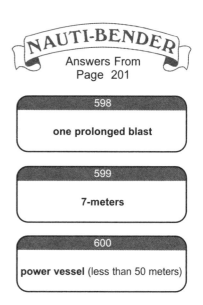

NAUTI-BENDER
Answers From
Page 201

598
one prolonged blast

599
7-meters

600
power vessel (less than 50 meters)

A "_____" light remains illuminated at all times when in use.

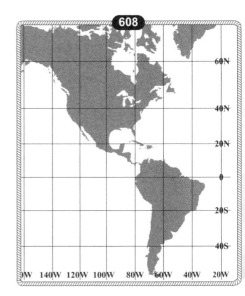

The most widely used coastal navigation charts utilize "_____" projection to produce parallels of latitude and meridians of longitude that intersect at right angles.

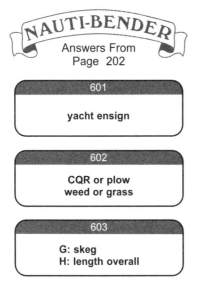

NAUTI-BENDER

Answers From
Page 202

601

yacht ensign

602

**CQR or plow
weed or grass**

603

**G: skeg
H: length overall**

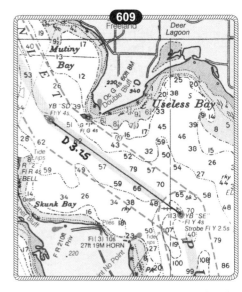

Traveling at 12 knots, using the dead reckoning formula (60D = ST): how long would it take to go from **YB "SE" to YB "SD"**?

Distances traveled on the Great Lakes system are typically expressed in: **kilometers**, **statute miles**, or **nautical miles**?

A "_____ _____" light flashes twice or more in regular intervals.

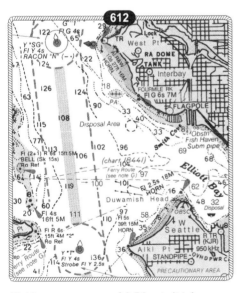

Making an average of 4.5 knots it takes you 67 minutes to travel from **Y "T" to Y "SG"**. What is the distance between the buoys (use dead reckoning formula: (60D = ST)?

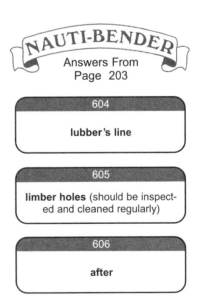

NAUTI-BENDER

Answers From
Page 203

604

lubber's line

605

limber holes (should be inspected and cleaned regularly)

606

after

613

You're on a collision course with a boat pulling a waterskier off your port bow. Who has the right-of-way?

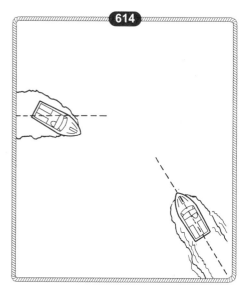

614

In a head-on, crossing, or overtaking situation, the burdened vessel should make its _____ known in an obvious and early fashion.

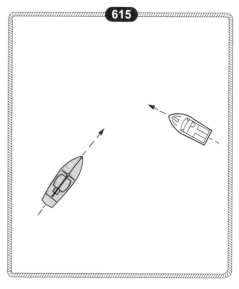

615

Which is the "**give way**" or "**burden**" vessel in the above situation?

A sailing vessel under sail is overtaking a powerboat. Which is the "give way" vessel?

The navigation rules are not explicit; however, it may be inferred that a boat emerging from a slip or berth **does** or **does not** have the right-of-way.

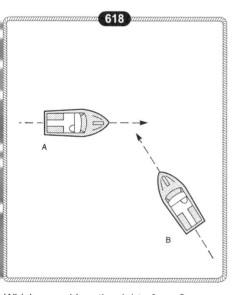

Which vessel has the right-of-way?

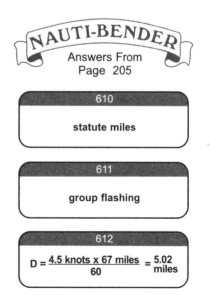

NAUTI-BENDER
Answers From
Page 205

610

statute miles

611

group flashing

612

$$D = \frac{4.5 \text{ knots} \times 67 \text{ miles}}{60} = 5.02 \text{ miles}$$

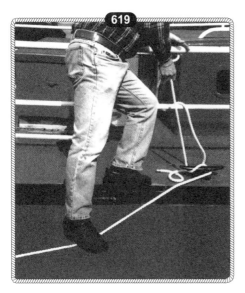

A dock line can be easily tightened or "_____ _____" by stepping down on the line, while "checked" at the cleat and then, in one quick motion, take up the slack while removing your foot.

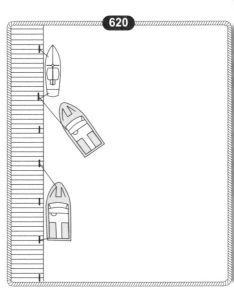

A _____ _____ line can be utilized to get into a tight slip with the engine slow _____ with the rudder hard _____.

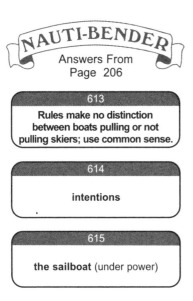

NAUTI-BENDER
Answers From Page 206

613
Rules make no distinction between boats pulling or not pulling skiers; use common sense.

614
intentions

615
the sailboat (under power)

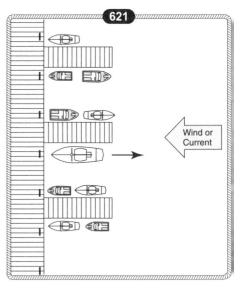

Wind or Current

Departing stern into wind (assuming single-screw boat): back out – the boat will back to _____ and clear pier nicely; or if poor reverse control, "walk the boat" out to end of pier.

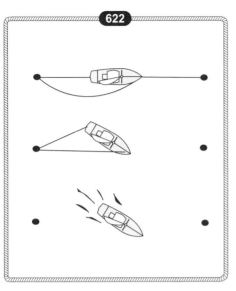

When tied-up between moorings or piles, stern-to wind or tide, a long bow line can be utilized to "_____" the stern out for easy departure.

When passing through a lock, which is the best side to moor to?

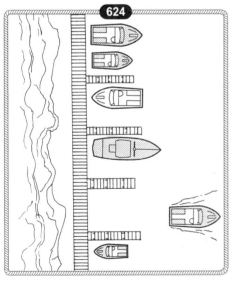

A twin-screw vessel (counter rotating propellers), with rudder amidships, and both engines backing will back _____.

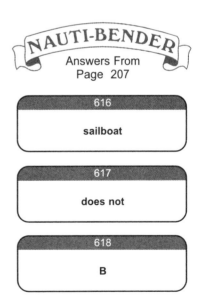

NAUTI-BENDER
Answers From
Page 207

616

sailboat

617

does not

618

B

625

A telltale attached to a shroud on a docked boat will indicate the **true** or **apparent** wind direction?

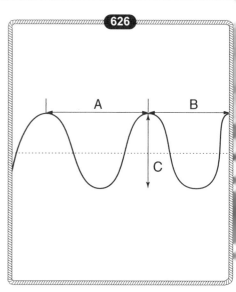

626

A wave's _____ is the distance from crest to crest ("**A**" above); it's _____ is the time between the two crests "**B**" above; its _____ is the distance from trough to crest ("**C**" above).

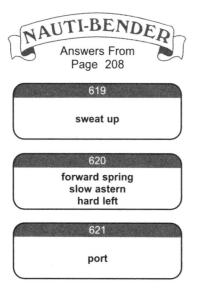

NAUTI-BENDER

Answers From
Page 208

619
sweat up

620
forward spring
slow astern
hard left

621
port

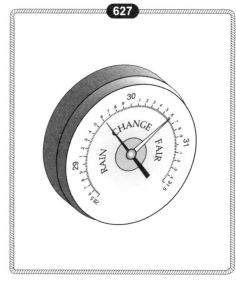

627

1. Falling barometer with winds from the East usually means _____ weather.
2. Rising barometer with winds from the West usually means _____ weather.

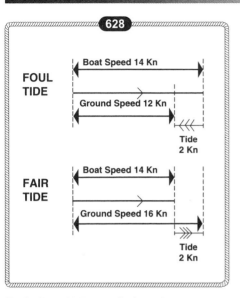

Typically, which usually has the strongest current: a **flood** or an **ebb tide**?

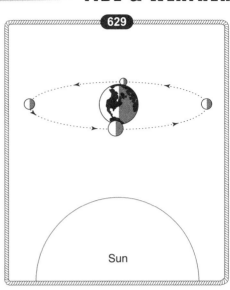

Spring tides (higher highs, lower lows) occur twice a month on the _____ and _____ moon.

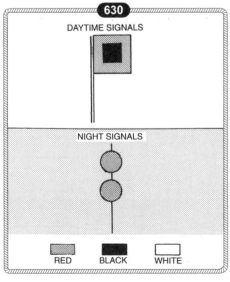

The above signal indicates a "_____" weather warning with winds between _____ and _____.

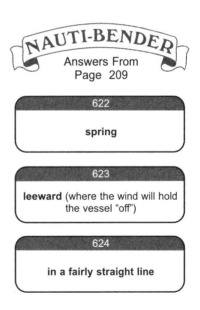

NAUTI-BENDER

Answers From
Page 209

622

spring

623

leeward (where the wind will hold the vessel "off")

624

in a fairly straight line

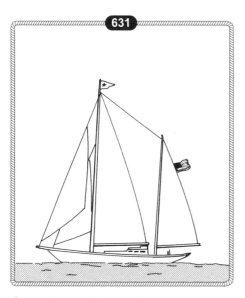

631

Generally speaking, a pleasure boat over _____ feet is referred to as a "yacht".

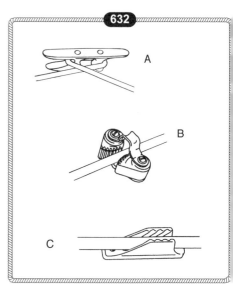

632

A

B

C

Identify the above deck gear.

NAUTI-BENDER
Answers From
Page 210

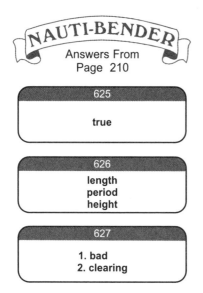

625

true

626

length
period
height

627

1. bad
2. clearing

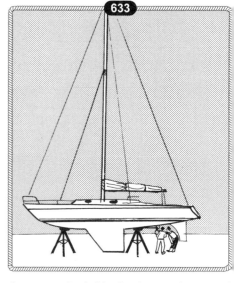

633

A person who is hired to inspect boats and ships before purchase is referred to as a marine "_____".

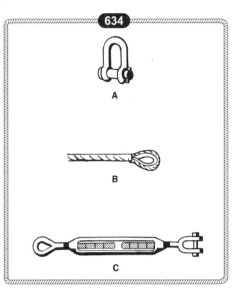

Identify the above.

To "_____" a vessel means to move it into a desired position by manipulating lines extended to shore, dock, another boat, etc.

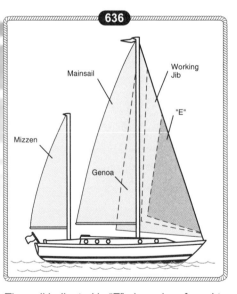

The sail indicated in "**E**" above is referred to as the "_____ _____".

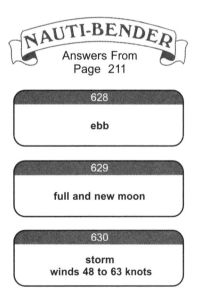

NAUTI-BENDER

Answers From
Page 211

628
ebb

629
full and new moon

630
storm **winds 48 to 63 knots**

637

Large ships can _____ the wind from unsuspecting sailors, leaving them without steerage when they need it most!

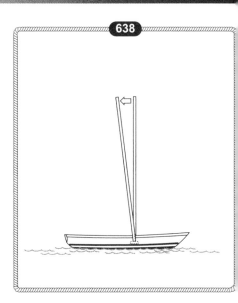

638

"Raking": bending the mast aft (2 degrees to 5 degrees) to change the shape of the mainsail normally done when sailing

_____ _____ _____ _____.

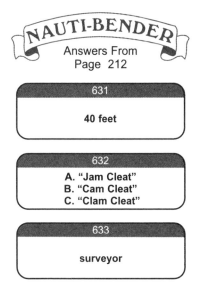

NAUTI-BENDER
Answers From
Page 212

631

40 feet

632

A. "Jam Cleat"
B. "Cam Cleat"
C. "Clam Cleat"

633

surveyor

639

If you have to run an inlet with a high, following sea (should be avoided if possible), one effective method is to ride in on the _____ of a wave.

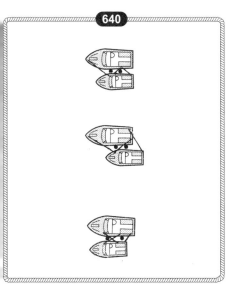

640

When towing alongside, the towboat's stern should be **even with**, **aft-of** or **forward-of** the other boat's transom for better control?

641

When aground on a falling tide, you must _____ _____ by heeling the boat over (sails or weight on extended boom or by positioning crew fore or aft).

642

Sailing toward an approaching thunderstorm (isolated, not part of a frontal system), the wind will become **stronger** or **weaker**?

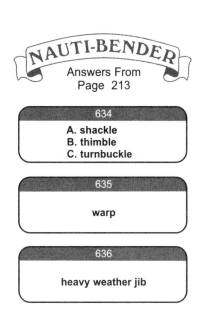

NAUTI-BENDER
Answers From
Page 213

634

A. shackle
B. thimble
C. turnbuckle

635

warp

636

heavy weather jib

Red daymarks have a _____ shape since the silhouette resembles the top of a _____ buoy and are _____ numbered.

Return to port from sea: "Red _____ returning".

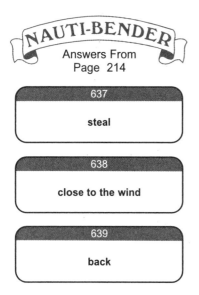

NAUTI-BENDER

Answers From
Page 214

637

steal

638

close to the wind

639

back

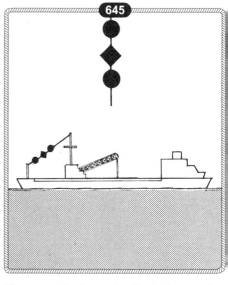

The vessel above is displaying a day shape indicating she is _____.

BUOYS & DAY SHAPES

646

A. 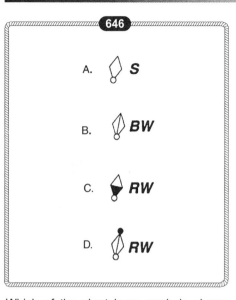 **S**

B. **BW**

C. **RW**

D. **RW**

Which of the chart buoy symbols shown above indicates a safe-water mark?

647

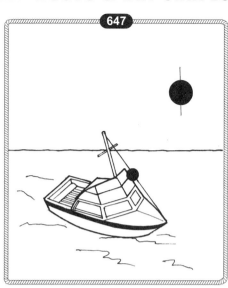

The vessel above is displaying a day shape indicating she is _____.

648

Entering an unfamiliar harbor at night, you note several lighted buoys flashing at different intervals. You are looking for a "morse" buoy cycling a _____ and _____ flash.

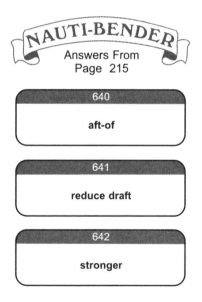

NAUTI-BENDER
Answers From
Page 215

640

aft-of

641

reduce draft

642

stronger

217

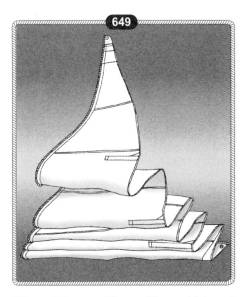

When storing a sail in a sail bag, which part of the sail is inserted first: the **foot**, **head**, or **clew**?

Before rendering assistance to another vessel, bear in mind: your first priority is to ensure your vessel does not _____ or _____ to the other vessel's problems.

NAUTI-BENDER
Answers From
Page 216

643
triangular **nun** **even** (like nunbuoys)

644
right

645
restricted in ability to maneuver

VHF radios have a working range of between _____ and _____ miles in ideal conditions.

In water skiing parlance: if one is "**skiing 15 off**", what does this mean?

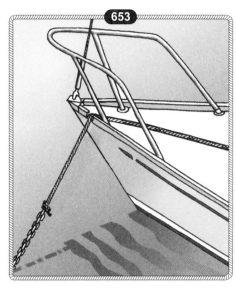

If the bitter end of your chain anchor rode is secured with a length of line that will reach topside, it can be easily _____ in the event of an emergency.

What is one of the most common causes of crew overboard and drowning?

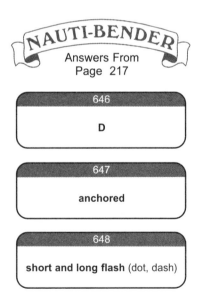

NAUTI-BENDER
Answers From
Page 217

646
D

647
anchored

648
short and long flash (dot, dash)

In an anchorage (light wind conditions)... why do powerboats and sailboats sometimes point in different directions?

Ripples flowing around a piling indicate the current's _____ and _____; if it's wet above the water line the tidal flow is _____ _____.

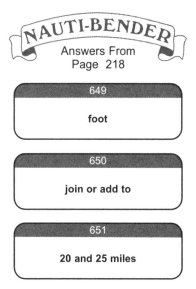

NAUTI-BENDER
Answers From Page 218

649
foot

650
join or add to

651
20 and 25 miles

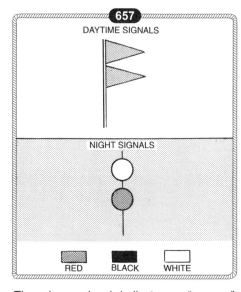

The above signal indicates a "_____" weather warning with winds between _____ and _____.

658

Buys Ballot's Law: while facing the "true" wind (northern hemisphere), the _____ of the storm will lie approximately 20 degrees behind your outstretched right arm.

659

In winter, when cold air (below 10 degrees) blows "off the land"... a steamy fog may form called "_____ _____".

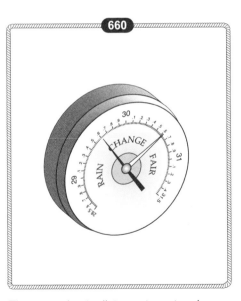

660

The approximate distance to a storm's center can be determined by noting a barometer's hourly rate of fall. Assuming a 0.08 – 0.12 inch/hour fall, what is the approximate distance to the storm's center?

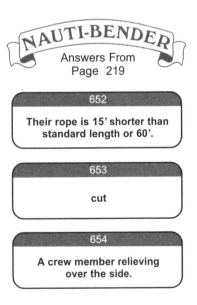

NAUTI-BENDER

Answers From
Page 219

652

Their rope is 15' shorter than standard length or 60'.

653

cut

654

A crew member relieving over the side.

Many factors determine a boat's maximum capacity. A rule-of-thumb safety loading formula is _____?

Safety Tip: always _____ the ignition key or _____ _____ the ignition system's power source before working around the engine or propeller.

Answers From
Page 220

655
Tidal flows have more or less effect on different keel configurations.

656
direction and strength going out ("ebbing")

657
gale winds 34-47 knots

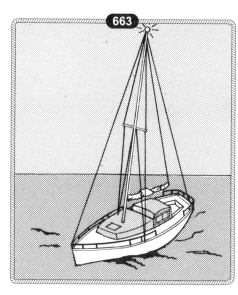

A distress signal or SOS can be done with a high-intensity light with **what series of dots and dashes**.

Which portable fire extinguisher should be protected from freezing temperatures... **foam**, **dry chemical**, or **C0₂**?

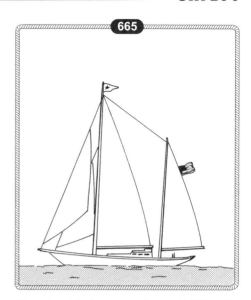

Every boat that operates beyond VHF radio range (20-25 miles) should carry an ___ ___ ___ ___ (EPIRB) and a single side-band radio for communications.

A propane fire is best extinguished by: **dousing with water**, **Type B** or **Type C extinguisher**, or **by shutting off fuel supply**.

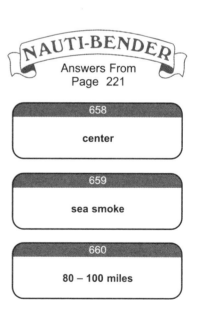

NAUTI-BENDER
Answers From
Page 221

658

center

659

sea smoke

660

80 – 100 miles

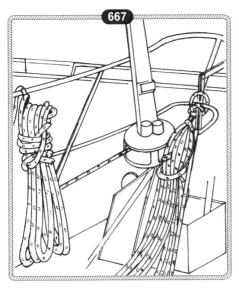

667

If your dock lines are becoming stiff due to age or exposure to the sun, try soaking them overnight in a liquid _____ _____.

668

The "_____ _____" knot is used as a stopper to prevent a line from running through a block or grommet.

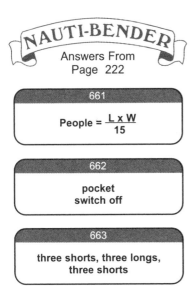

NAUTI-BENDER
Answers From
Page 222

661
People = $\dfrac{L \times W}{15}$

662
pocket switch off

663
three shorts, three longs, three shorts

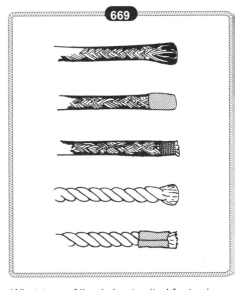

669

What type of line is best suited for towing a disabled vessel: **polypropylene**, **dacron**, **hemp**, **three-strand nylon**, or **double-braided nylon**?

670

The most popular method of attaching a line to a spar, stachion, or ring is with two "_____ _____."

671

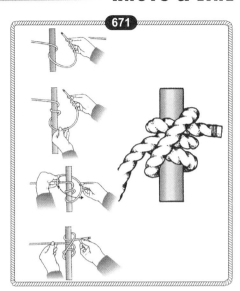

The rolling hitch is unique in that when tied to a verticle object (mast, stanchion line, or cable), it won't slip downward under strain and can easily be adjusted _____.

672

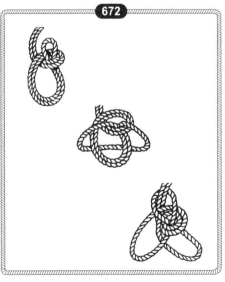

A substitute "boatswain's chair" (to recover a man overboard or for going aloft) can be readily fashioned by a "_____ _____ _____ _____."

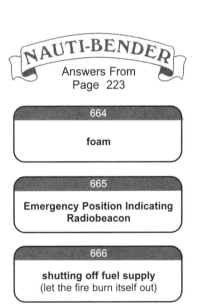

NAUTI-BENDER
Answers From
Page 223

664

foam

665

Emergency Position Indicating Radiobeacon

666

shutting off fuel supply
(let the fire burn itself out)

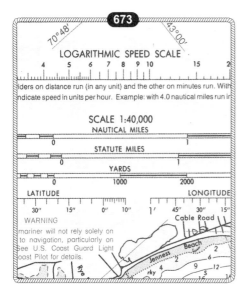

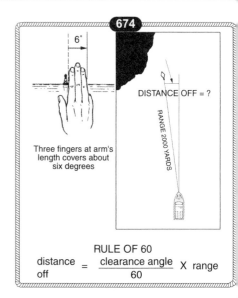

Yards-Per-Minute Rule: in one minute a vessel making three knots will cover 100 yards. What distance (miles) will a vessel making 15 knots travel in four minutes?

The **"Rule of 60"** equates that an angle of six degrees will give a clearance of 1/10 the range. In the above example, if you steered six degrees to the right of the direct bearing to the buoy, what would the **distance off** be?

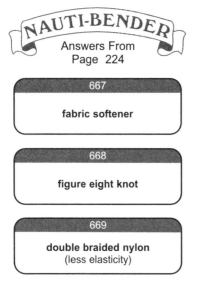

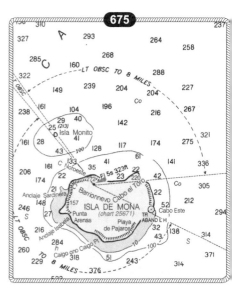

Underway in a small boat at night, you intermittently observe a light (ISLA de MONA Lighthouse) on the horizon. The approximate distance to the lighthouse would be **15**, **20**, or **25** miles?

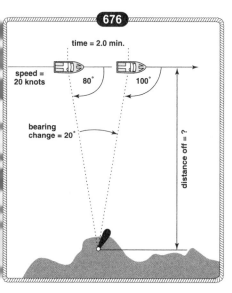

676

Using the "angle = speed" method shown above, determine "distance off" where distance off = time.

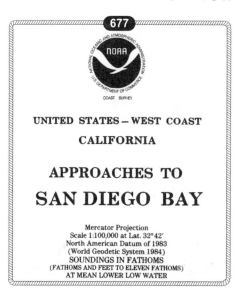

677

A scale of 1:100,000 on a NOAA Chart indicates that 1 inch on the chart equals:
(A) **100,000 miles**, (B) **100,000 yards**, (C) **100,000 inches**, or (D) **100,000 feet** on earth.

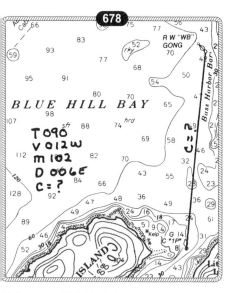

678

Using the "TVMCD" formula, convert true course 090 degrees in the above example to a compass course.

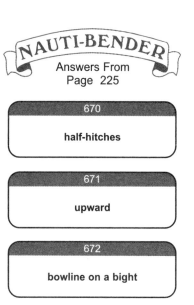

NAUTI-BENDER
Answers From
Page 225

670

half-hitches

671

upward

672

bowline on a bight

679

Approaching a channel inlet on a flood tide, you observe an onshore wind and five-foot rollers at the mouth. You should ride: (A) **on the back**, (B) **in front of**, or (C) **on the crest** of a roller and take it in.

680

The boat will have better maneuverability when the tow rope is secured well _____ of the transom.

NAUTI-BENDER
Answers From
Page 226

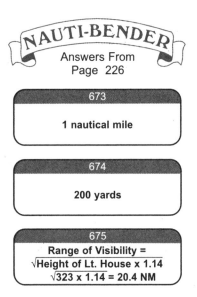

673
1 nautical mile

674
200 yards

675
Range of Visibility = $\sqrt{\text{Height of Lt. House}} \times 1.14$
$\sqrt{323} \times 1.14 = 20.4$ NM

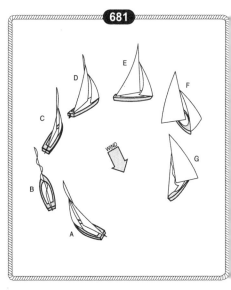

681

A sailing vessel with the wind coming from 089° relative would be: **close hauled (starboard tack)**, **reaching (starboard tack)**, **broad reach (starboard tack)**, or **close hauled (port tack)**.

A "towing bridle" is used... **for more control**; **to distribute the strain equally**; or **to reduce the amount of power** required for the tow?

While going ahead on twin engines (rudders amidships) your port engine stalls. To continue on course you should: **apply right rudder**, **apply left rudder**, **keep rudders amidships**, or **increase engine speed**.

You are running a twin-screw vessel going ahead with rudders amidships; if the port engine suddenly stops the boat will: **go to port**, **go to starboard**, **continue on a straight course**.

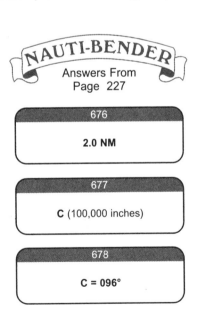

NAUTI-BENDER
Answers From
Page 227

676
2.0 NM

677
C (100,000 inches)

678
C = 096°

It is usually good practice for smaller vessels to enter a lock _____ and then raft alongside larger vessels, thus minimizing line-handling/fending-off efforts.

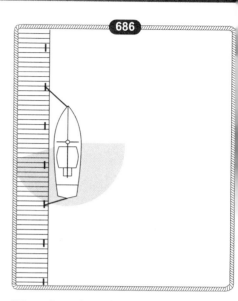

When departing, with wind aft of the beam (as shown above), leave **bow** or **stern** first.

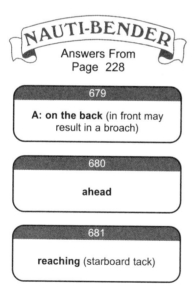

NAUTI-BENDER
Answers From
Page 228

679

A: **on the back** (in front may result in a broach)

680

ahead

681

reaching (starboard tack)

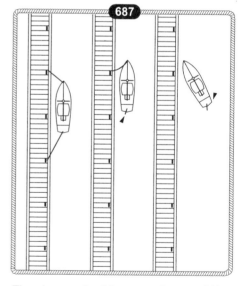

The above unberthing procedure would be proper with the wind coming _____ _____ _____.

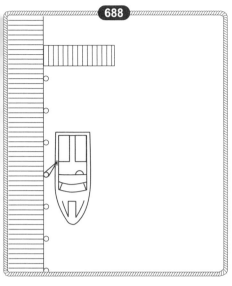

688

Departures from pilings are made easier by securing _____ ends of the spring line at the boat.

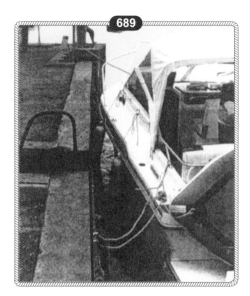

689

The vessel shown above is docked bow into a tidal flow or current. Utilization of **which dock line** would have prevented the bow from being pushed in?

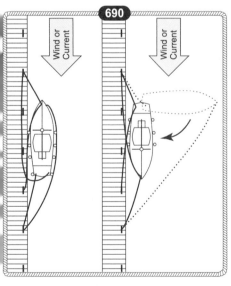

690

At the dock, turning the boat by hand using lines would most easily be accomplished (in the above situation) with the wind or tidal flow coming from **ahead** or **astern**?

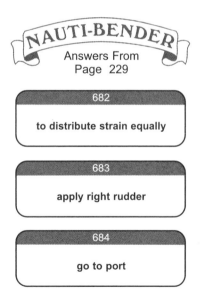

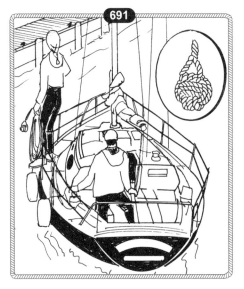

691

The round ball on the end of a heaving line is called a "_____ _____".

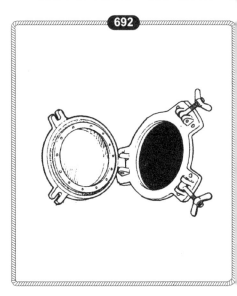

692

Nautical windows are properly called "_____" when they **cannot** be opened, and "_____" when they **can** be opened.

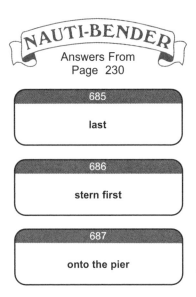

NAUTI-BENDER
Answers From
Page 230

685

last

686

stern first

687

onto the pier

693

When waterskiers say they are skiing "22 off", how long is their ski rope?

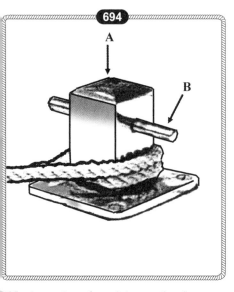

694

"**A**" above is referred to as the "_____ _____" and "**B**" is the "_____ _____".

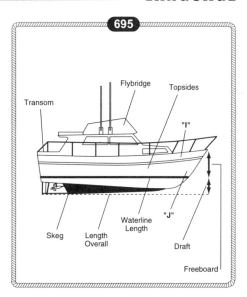

695

Flybridge
Topsides
Transom
"I"
Skeg
Length Overall
Waterline Length
"J"
Draft
Freeboard

Hull language: "**I**" and "**J**" (shown above) would be referred to as the "_____" and "_____".

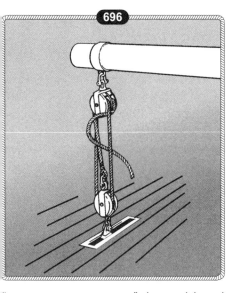

696

"_____ _____ _____", is a quick and simple method of temporarily "jamming" or stopping all movement of a line through a block.

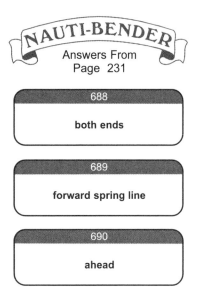

NAUTI-BENDER
Answers From
Page 231

688

both ends

689

forward spring line

690

ahead

When boarding a dinghy, step aft if some-one is forward, forward if someone is aft – but always step on the "_____" of the boat.

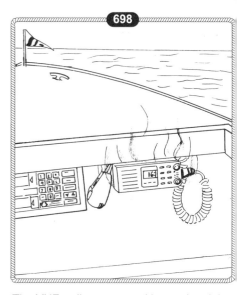

The VHF radio starts smoking and emitting sparks... what should the skipper's first action be?

In an emergency, diesel engines can be run completely underwater, provided the **fuel supply**, **battery** or **air intake** is above water?

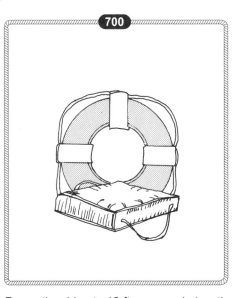

700

Recreational boats 16 ft. or more in length must have on board at least one Type IV "_____" PFD.

701

Halon gas will decompose and may form very hazardous toxic fumes when discharged: **directly on the flames**, **in extremely cold temperatures**, or **at room temperature**.

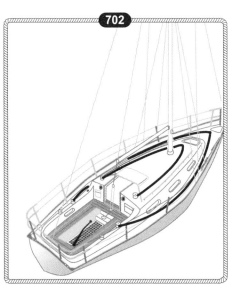

702

When wearing a safety harness, rig "jack lines" and always use a tether that is as short as possible, snapped onto the boat's **windward** (uphill) or **leeward** (downhill) side (never to the center).

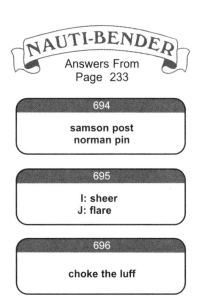

NAUTI-BENDER
Answers From
Page 233

694

samson post
norman pin

695

I: sheer
J: flare

696

choke the luff

703

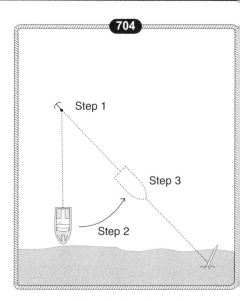

704

Step 1

Step 3

Step 2

Anchor stuck: take a strain on anchor line (attach float), then tie a bowline or another line and let it slip down around anchor; pull release line in _____ direction.

Assuming light winds and sufficient room, the above anchoring technique is simply executed and especially useful in a _____ tide situation.

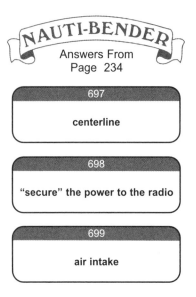

NAUTI-BENDER
Answers From
Page 234

697

centerline

698

"secure" the power to the radio

699

air intake

705

To prevent an anchor from dragging in heavy weather a "_____" should be rigged.

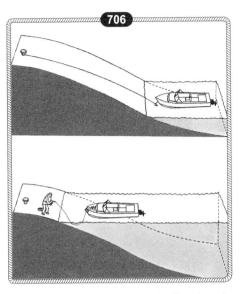

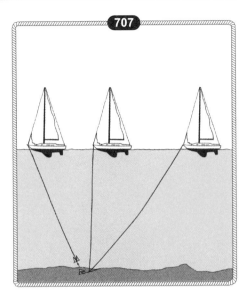

Retrieving a boat anchored off a beach, with a flood tide is easily accomplished by rigging a "_____ _____" to the head of the anchor and proceeding as shown above.

If the anchor won't break loose: cleat the rode when directly over the anchor, then proceed slowly on **the same** or **the opposite** course used initially when setting the anchor, until it breaks free.

Anchoring final step: the _____ should inspect the foredeck to ensure the anchor rode is properly cleated/stowed and proper chafing gear has been installed.

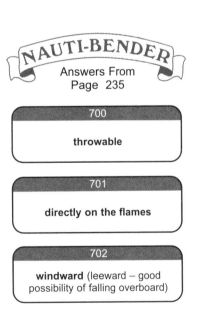

NAUTI-BENDER
Answers From
Page 235

700

throwable

701

directly on the flames

702

windward (leeward – good possibility of falling overboard)

When underway at night, avoid using white lights (they will temporarily impair your "night vision"). Recovery from exposure to a bright light may take up to _____ minutes.

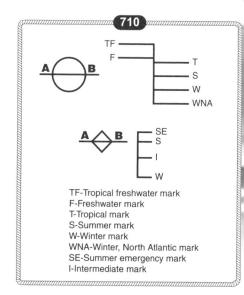

TF-Tropical freshwater mark
F-Freshwater mark
T-Tropical mark
S-Summer mark
W-Winter mark
WNA-Winter, North Atlantic mark
SE-Summer emergency mark
I-Intermediate mark

The upper "plimsoll" mark is used when the vessel is on the _____, and the lower is used when the vessel is on the _____ _____.

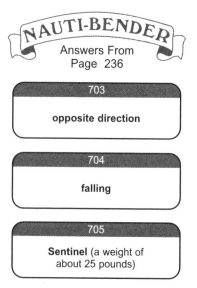

The water-ski hand-signal shown above indicates: _____.

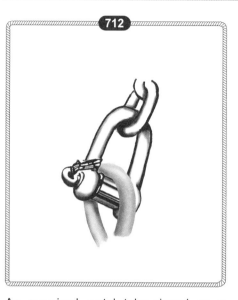

An oversized metal tube rigged on a _____ pin will revolve, reducing wear and tear.

To determine the torque your engine is producing at any one point in time, you need to know the engine's: (A) **RPMs**, (B) **horsepower**, (C) **compression ratio**, and/or (D) **bore & stroke**.

Which of the Great Lakes lies entirely within the United States: **Ontario**, **Michigan** or **Superior**?

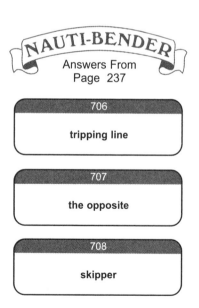

NAUTI-BENDER
Answers From
Page 237

706
tripping line

707
the opposite

708
skipper

715

Ketches and yawls typically carry light-weight mizzen staysails used on _____-wind legs.

716

"_____ _____" spinnakers stretch main-ly at the head and are best suited for down-wind sailing.

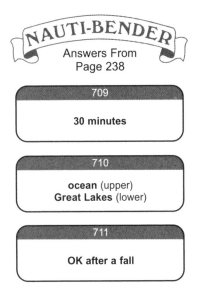
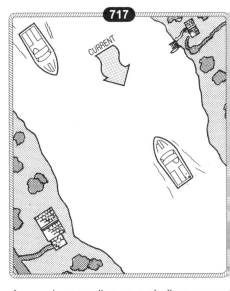

717

CURRENT

A vessel proceeding up a shallow, narrow channel may experience "bank cushion". This phenomenon will force the **bow** or **stern** – **away** or **toward** the nearest bank.

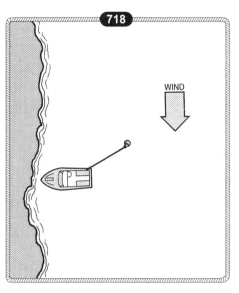

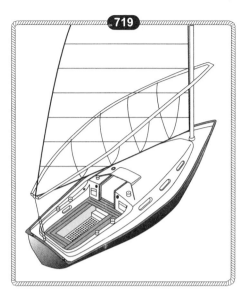

If your boat has gone aground and the tide is falling... the best action you can take is to set out a "_____" anchor.

The "_____" rig shown above automatically keeps the leech firm, typically eliminating the need for a "_____ _____" or a large tackle on the "_____ _____."

When fog develops, it is a good practice that all crew and passengers don lifejackets; also have _____ and a _____ ready for use in an emergency.

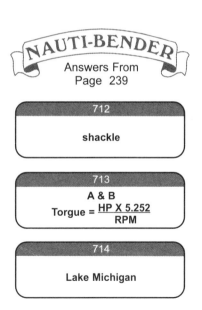

NAUTI-BENDER
Answers From
Page 239

712
shackle

713
A & B
Torgue = $\dfrac{\text{HP X 5.252}}{\text{RPM}}$

714
Lake Michigan

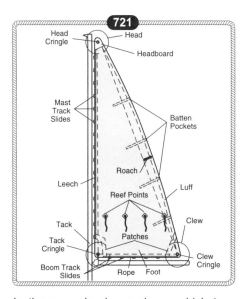

In the example shown above, which **two** descriptors have been transposed?

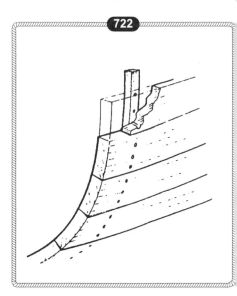

"_____" construction: a method of boat building in which the side planks are butt together flush and the seams caulked to make a smooth finish.

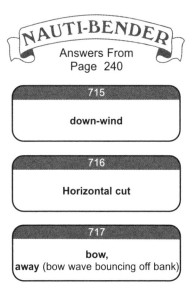

NAUTI-BENDER

Answers From
Page 240

715

down-wind

716

Horizontal cut

717

bow,
away (bow wave bouncing off bank)

COWL

A "_____" vent allows air below while blocking incoming spray. In rough weather the "cowl" should be turned **forward** or **aft**?

724

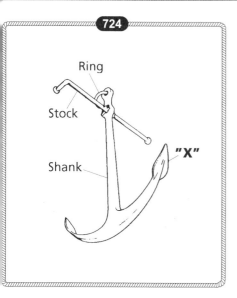

Ring

Stock

Shank

"X"

Anchor Nomenclature: "**X**" shown above would be referred to as the "_____".

725

A "_____ _____": lines rigged on both sides of the mainsail so when lowered, the sail will gather automatically to the boom.

726

The direction and force the wind seems to have when observed from a vessel in motion is referred to as _____ _____.

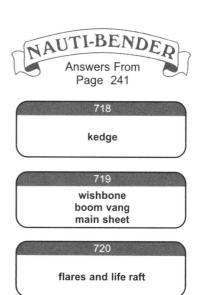

NAUTI-BENDER

Answers From
Page 241

718

kedge

719

wishbone
boom vang
main sheet

720

flares and life raft

After washing down the boat, pouring the excess soapy water into the bilge accomplishes two objectives: helps keep the bilge clean, plus _____ any minor amounts of fuel or engine oil that may have accumulated.

If your outboard engine should fall overboard and is retrieved, it should be stored _____ until several hours before being repaired.

NAUTI-BENDER
Answers From Page 242

721

leech shoul be luff
and vice versa

722

carvel

723

dorade
aft

Smoke from exhaust (diesel engine): a faulty injector (excessive fuel) or an overloaded engine will produce _____ smoke.

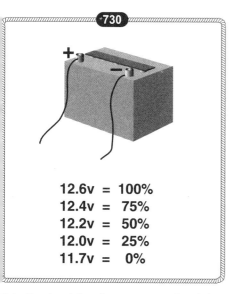

12.6v = 100%
12.4v = 75%
12.2v = 50%
12.0v = 25%
11.7v = 0%

A battery's state of _____ can be determined by utilizing an accurate voltmeter as delineated above.

Assuming you're cruising offshore and lose hydraulic steering oil, which fluid can be temporarily substituted: **fresh water**, **sea water**, **beer** or **all of the above**?

First golden rule of working on inboard engines: lay cloth or blanket under work area to prevent dropped _____ and _____ from falling into the bilge.

NAUTI-BENDER
Answers From
Page 243

724

fluke

725

lazy jack

726

apparent wind

Cruising at night you observe a flashing amber light (three-second intervals) indicating the presence of a _____?

A bell is used to sound a fog signal for vessels at _____ or _____.

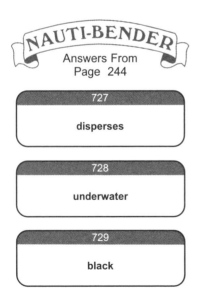

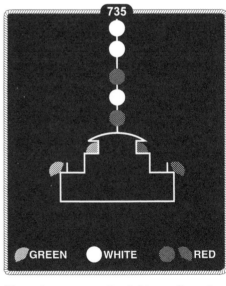

GREEN WHITE RED

The above vessel's light configuration would indicate she is _____.

While cruising in fog, you hear a sound signal ahead (a long blast followed by three short blasts) indicating a vessel being towed and _____.

Which waterborne vessel(s) is/are not required to display a specific arrangement of red, green, or white lights: (A) **seaplanes**, (B) **submarines**, (C) **air-cushion boats** and/or (D) **cruising cars**?

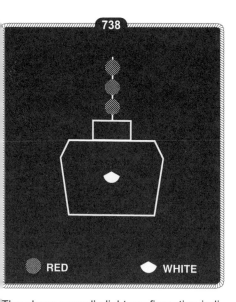

RED   WHITE

The above vessel's light configuration indicates what?

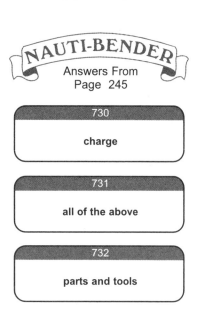

739

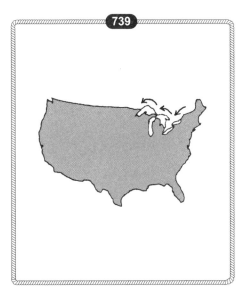

"Returning from seaward" in general, is considered to be Northerly and Westerly in the Great Lakes except southerly in Lake _____.

740

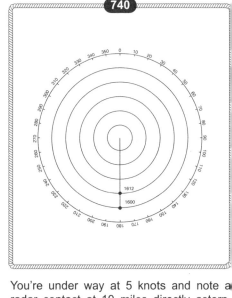

You're under way at 5 knots and note a radar contact at 10 miles directly astern. Twelve minutes later the contact is directly astern at eight miles – what is contact's speed?

741

Before getting under way, your Loran-C or GPS receiver should be checked for accuracy. Save a way point at your launching ramp or slip – when checked, the distance should be between 0.0 to _____ miles.

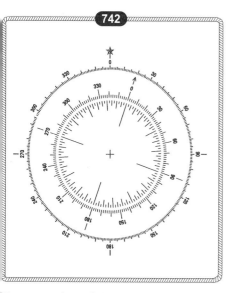

The outer ring of the compass rose indicates: _____ direction, the inner ring indicates _____ direction, and the innermost ring indicates compass "_____".

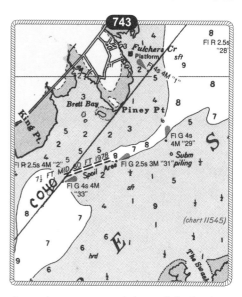

Assuming your vessel draws 3 feet, when would you schedule your sightseeing trip to Piney Point?

Small craft warnings refer to vessels under _____ meters.

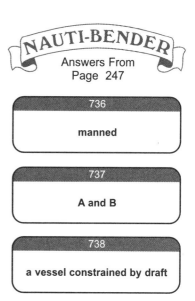

NAUTI-BENDER

Answers From
Page 247

736
manned

737
A and B

738
a vessel constrained by draft

745

While some I/O's may steer a little sluggishly at _____ speeds, they are great for "_____" your way out of a tight slip (the hull will "follow" the prop.

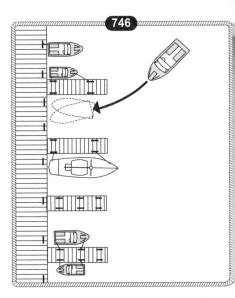

746

When docking a single-screw vessel (right-hand propeller) starboard side-to: if you back down to stop the boat's forward motion with the rudder amidships, you would expect the bow to turn **toward** or **away** from the dock?

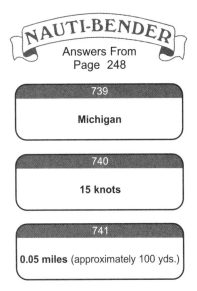

NAUTI-BENDER
Answers From
Page 248

739
Michigan

740
15 knots

741
0.05 miles (approximately 100 yds.)

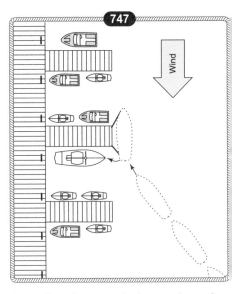

747

Wind

Assuming the vessel shown above has poor control in reverse, maneuver to the end of the slip (bow into wind), secure with lines, then the crew can "_____" the boat in.

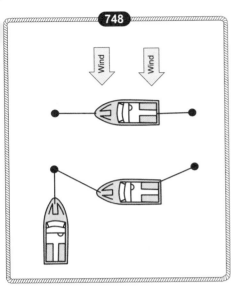

Moored between moorings or piles side-to a gale: reduce strain on mooring lines by _____ _____ both lines; or better yet, if leeway exists, let go the _____ line and lie head into the wind.

While docking, a line handler inadvertently drops a line in the water. What should the skipper do first?

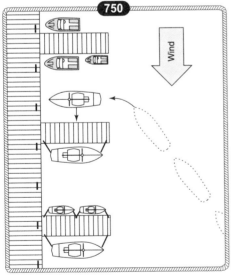

Docking in a windward slip: put in neutral and coast in, apply short burst astern, or rig a _____ _____ to stop the boat's forward motion and let the wind move you gently alongside.

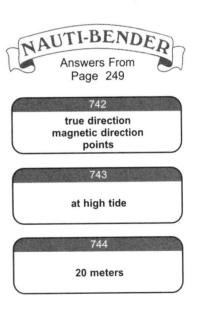

NAUTI-BENDER
Answers From
Page 249

742
true direction
magnetic direction
points

743
at high tide

744
20 meters

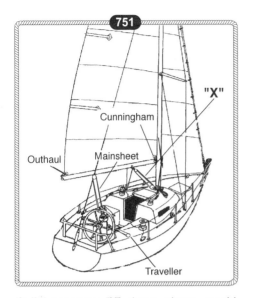

751

"X"

Cunningham

Outhaul Mainsheet

Traveller

Sail Language: "**X**" shown above, would be referred to as the "_____ _____", which is used to pull the boom down and adjust the leech of the main sail.

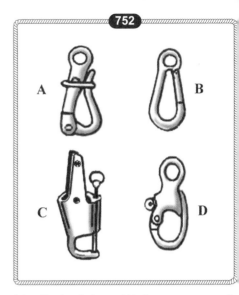

752

A

B

C

D

Identify the fittings: (**A**) "_____ _____", (**B**) "_____ _____", (**C**) "_____ _____", and (**D**) "_____ _____" shown above.

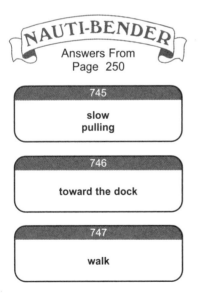

NAUTI-BENDER

Answers From
Page 250

745

slow
pulling

746

toward the dock

747

walk

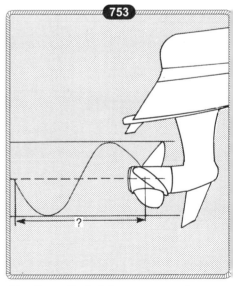

753

?

The theoretical distance a vessel moves forward with each prop revolution is referred to as "_____".

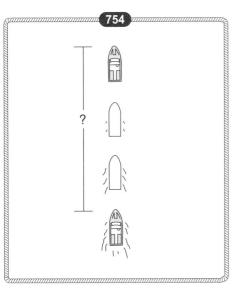

754

The distance a vessel will travel from the time the engine(s) is/are put full astern until it is dead in the water is referred to as "_____ _____".

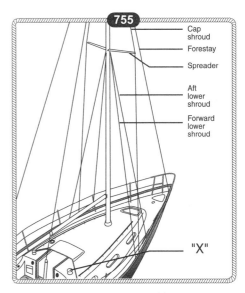

755

Cap shroud
Forestay
Spreader
Aft lower shroud
Forward lower shroud
"X"

Sail Language: "**X**" shown above, would be referred to as the _____ _____ _____.

756

The above vessel is referred to as a "_____".

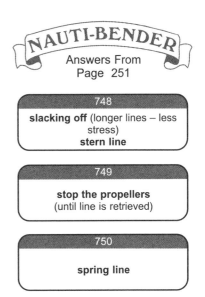

NAUTI-BENDER
Answers From
Page 251

748

slacking off (longer lines – less stress)
stern line

749

stop the propellers
(until line is retrieved)

750

spring line

757

If your dock line is not quite long enough to tie up in the traditional manner, a _____ hitch and "slippery" _____ hitch can be utilized as shown above.

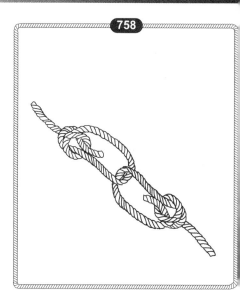

758

A "_____" can be used to quickly join two lines.

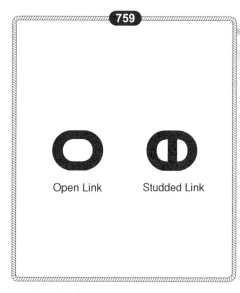

759

Open Link   Studded Link

Chain "links" are either open or studded. "Studding" prevents the chain from _____ and increases its strength by _____%.

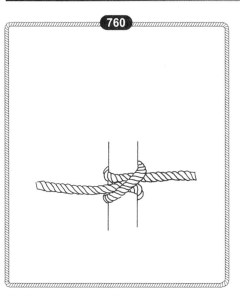

The "_____ _____" is useful for securing a line to a piling or ring when terminated with one or two half-hitches.

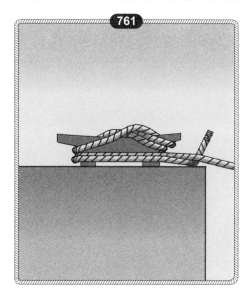

Prevent the edge of the dock from chafing your lines on an ebbing tide by wrapping the excess (after cleating) _____ the standing part.

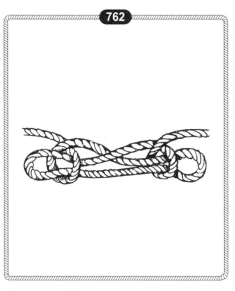

Sheepshank is a knot commonly used by lobstermen to _____ a line.

763

Before attempting a night passage, ensure the captain is experienced and the crew can perform all necessary shipboard routines in the _____.

764

When retrieving a person who has fallen overboard: you should approach from the **windward** or **leeward**?

765

Assuming your vessel has no power and is rolling in a heavy sea – you may reduce the possibility of capsizing by rigging a "_____" or "_____".

Sail trimming must satisfy two goals: keep the boat sailing _____ and in _____.

Cruising in fog, **always** or **never** stand on your right-of-way per the rules of the road.

Which is more likely to cause a vessel to capsize – **running into head seas**, **in the trough**, or **with a following sea**?

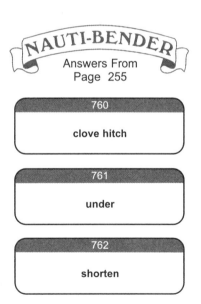

NAUTI-BENDER
Answers From Page 255

760
clove hitch

761
under

762
shorten

Boat Trailering: too much weight on the tongue will: (A) **put undue strain on tow vehicle's suspension**; (B) **make the vehicle hard to steer**; (C) **likely make the trailer "fishtale";** or (D) **all of the above**.

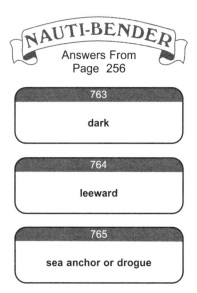

NAUTI-BENDER
Answers From
Page 256

763

dark

764

leeward

765

sea anchor or drogue

Spinnaker sheets should be _____ the length of the boat and the genoa sheets should be _____ and _____ its length.

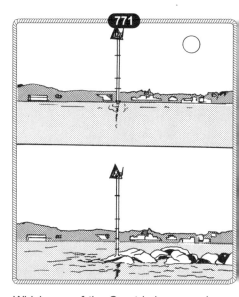

Which one of the Great Lakes experience the least amount of seasonal high- and low-water fluctuations: **Huron**, **Erie**, **Superior** or **Michigan**?

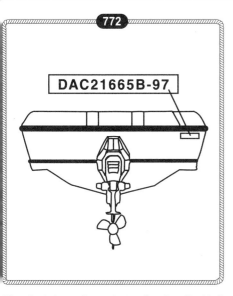

The last two characters of a boat's **H**ull **I**dentification **N**umber (HIN) indicates the _____ the boat was built.

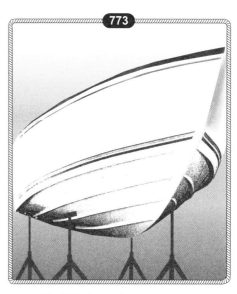

A modified-V hull requires more power than a flat-bottomed boat but less than a full _____-_____ hull design.

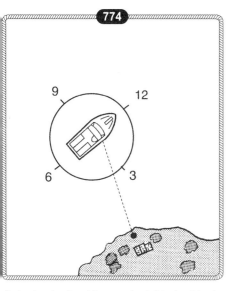

A lookout should report sighted objects using: (A) **true**, (B) **magnetic**, (C) **relative bearings**, or (D) **clock notation system**.

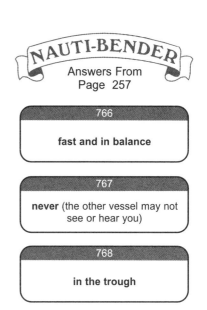

NAUTI-BENDER
Answers From
Page 257

766

fast and in balance

767

never (the other vessel may not see or hear you)

768

in the trough

It is illegal to discharge raw sewage from a vessel into any U.S. territorial waters within _____ miles of shore.

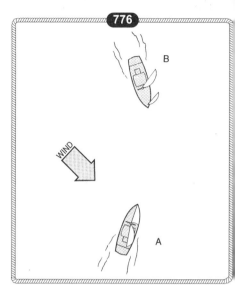

Which boat (above diagram) has the right-of-way?

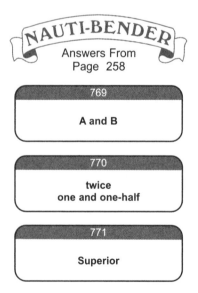

NAUTI-BENDER
Answers From
Page 258

769

A and B

770

**twice
one and one-half**

771

Superior

"General Prudential Rule"... if all else fails, the rules-of-the-road – **must be obeyed** or **may be broken** to avoid immediate danger.

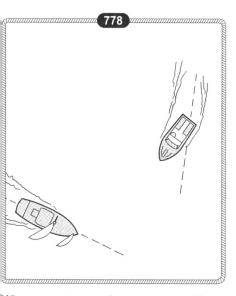

778

When a power vessel encounters a sailboat under sail – the _____ boat must give way and maneuver clear of the other.

779

Anchoring etiquette: first _____, first _____; should two vessels swing together, the responsibility lies with the vessel that anchored _____.

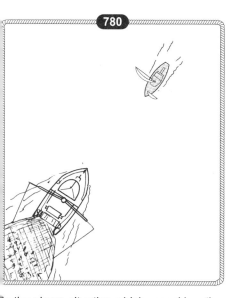

780

In the above situation which vessel has the right-of-way or is "privileged"?

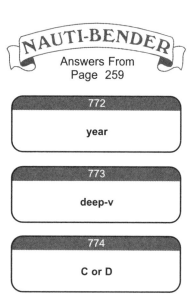

NAUTI-BENDER
Answers From
Page 259

772

year

773

deep-v

774

C or D

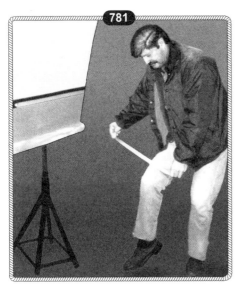

781

" _____ _____": a narrow strip of paint or tape of contrasting color applied between the "bottom" and "topside" paint that typically indicates the vessels natural _____.

782

When a vessel is set off course from a quartering sea, it is referred to as "_____".

NAUTI-BENDER
Answers From
Page 260

775

three

776

B

777

may be broken

783

Early ships used leadlines marked at inter-mittent intervals (2,3,5,7,10, etc.). If an estimate (based on nearest mark) was made, the leadsman would call out "deep..." – thus the modern-day term "deep _____".

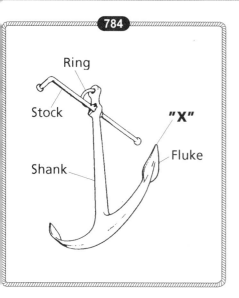

784

Ring

Stock

"**X**"

Shank

Fluke

Anchor Nomenclature: "**X**" shown above would be referred to as the "_____".

785

When being towed, it is good practice to periodically reduce the tow rope's length to avoid chafing; known as "_____ _____ _____".

786

To "_____" a line means to secure it to a cleat.

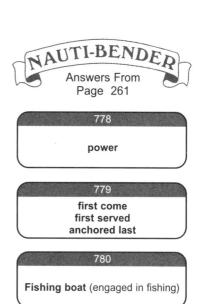

NAUTI-BENDER
Answers From
Page 261

778

power

779

**first come
first served
anchored last**

780

Fishing boat (engaged in fishing)

The color scheme of above cardinal buoy (Canada) indicates that a vessel must pass: **North**, **South**, **East**, or **West** of the buoy?

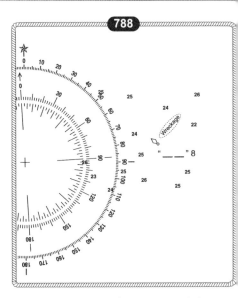

Wreck buoys are red or green and the regular number sequence is preceded by a "_____".

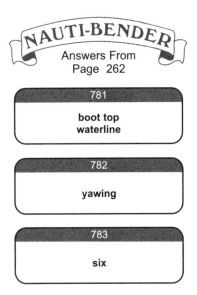

NAUTI-BENDER
Answers From
Page 262

781

boot top
waterline

782

yawing

783

six

You are entering an east coast port and see a buoy with a yellow triangle painted on it... indicating?

The vessel above is displaying a day shape indicating she is _____.

As defined by the U.S. Aids to Navigations System, speherical buoys may be: **numbered**, **lettered**, **lighted**, or **all of the above**.

Leaving the harbor, remember "red left _____."

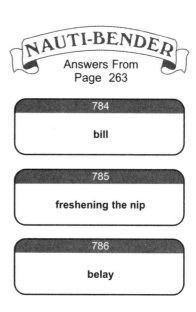

NAUTI-BENDER
Answers From
Page 263

784
bill

785
freshening the nip

786
belay

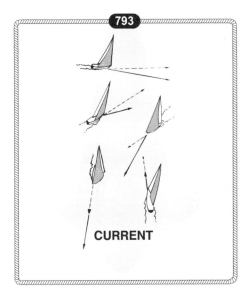

CURRENT

Currents at a 45° angle to the bow and stern affect course and speed at _____-_____ the velocity for each.

Small craft warnings are set when the wind speed is between _____ and _____ knots.

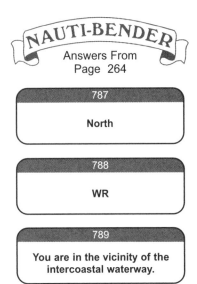

NAUTI-BENDER
Answers From
Page 264

787
North

788
WR

789
You are in the vicinity of the intercoastal waterway.

"When a halo rings the moon or sun the rain will come upon _____ _____".

796

AUGUST

Morning	Boston	Afternoon
HIGH 4:11 Height 9.8 LOW 10:18 Height 0.2 Sunrise 4:50	SUNDAY **14** FIRST QUARTER	HIGH 4:34 Height 10.8 LOW 11:00 Height -0.1 Sunset 6:47
HIGH 5:13 Height 9.4 LOW 11:17 Height 0.5 Sunrise 4:51	MONDAY **15**	HIGH 5:36 Height 10.7 LOW ——— Height ——— Sunset 6:46
HIGH 6:18 Height 9.2 LOW 12:04 Height 0.0 Sunrise 4:52	TUESDAY **16**	HIGH 6:39 Height 10.7 LOW 12:19 Height 0.7 Sunset 6:44
HIGH 7:24 Height 9.3 LOW 1:08 Height 0.0 Sunrise 4:53	WEDNESDAY **17**	HIGH 7:43 Height 10.7 LOW 1:22 Height 0.7 Sunset 6:43
HIGH 8:26 Height 9.4 LOW 2:09 Height -0.1 Sunrise 4:54	THURSDAY **18**	HIGH 8:43 Height 10.8 LOW 2:23 Height 0.5 Sunset 6:41
HIGH 9:23 Height 9.7 LOW 3:06 Height -0.3 Sunrise 4:55	FRIDAY **19**	HIGH 9:38 Height 10.9 LOW 3:19 Height 0.3 Sunset 6:40

Tide tables are sometimes shown in "standard time". To correct for daylight savings time, remember: "spring _____, fall _____."

797

Fog forms when the temperature and the _____ are the same.

798

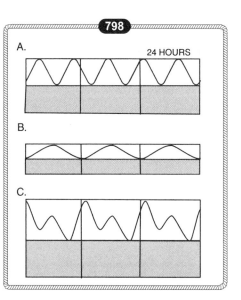

The above tidal range diagrams illustrate: "**A**" _____-_____tides, "**B**" _____ tides and "**C**" _____ tides.

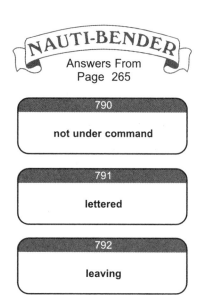

NAUTI-BENDER

Answers From
Page 265

790

not under command

791

lettered

792

leaving

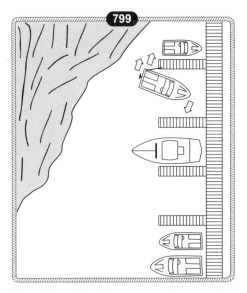

Departing with little room astern can be made easy, utilizing a short back spring with engine(s) _____ _____ and rudder _____.

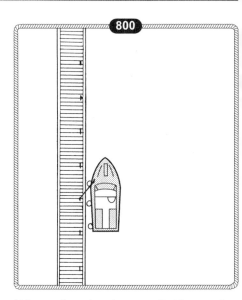

When going ahead on an after bow spring line (rudder amidships): the stern will go _____ and the bow will go _____.

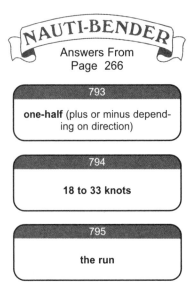

NAUTI-BENDER
Answers From Page 266

793

one-half (plus or minus depending on direction)

794

18 to 33 knots

795

the run

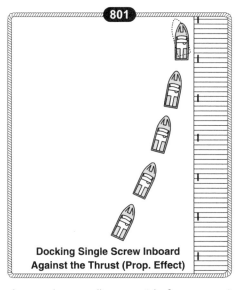

Docking Single Screw Inboard Against the Thrust (Prop. Effect)

Approach normally, except before you get to the stopping point, apply a short burst of power **forward** or **astern** to get the stern swinging to _____, then apply a short burst **forward** or **astern** to stop.

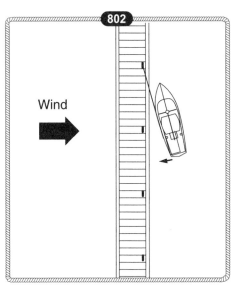

In the above spring-line docking scenario, the engine should be in _____ and the rudder hard _____.

When departing a fore- and aft-mooring, tie the _____ together for easy retrieval.

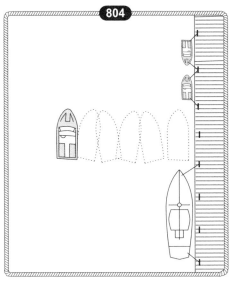

"Walking" sideways with twin-engines: apply hard _____ rudder with alternating short bursts of power forward and astern on the _____ engine until you reach the pier, then use the _____ engine to bring bow or stern in.

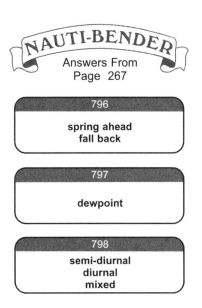

NAUTI-BENDER
Answers From
Page 267

796
spring ahead
fall back

797
dewpoint

798
semi-diurnal
diurnal
mixed

When a large ship proceeds up a relatively confined and shallow (in respect to the ship's draft) waterway, a _____ _____ is created which can violently rock the boats moored along its path.

Proper "trim" can be achieved in the boat shown above by tilting the drive **back** or **foward**?

When towing another vessel, the tow rope should be... **as long as possible**, **as short as possible**, or **be such that the vessels are "in-step"**.

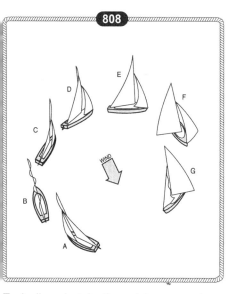

Typically, what is the minimum angle a close-hauled boat can "point" into the wind: **35°**, **45°**, or **50°**?

More or **less** driving force is achieved by heeling the boat over in heavy air, allowing the wind to spill over the top of the sail.

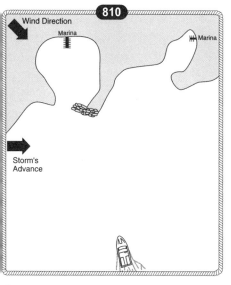

Caught in a sudden storm, one option (assuming time availability) would include _____ _____ of the storm to safety.

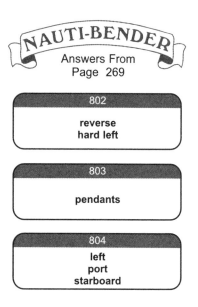

NAUTI-BENDER
Answers From
Page 269

802
reverse **hard left**

803
pendants

804
left **port** **starboard**

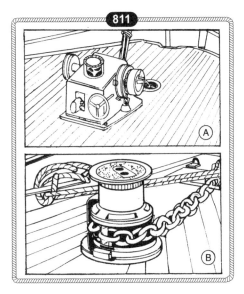

The "windlass" is "_____" shown above.
The "capstan" is "_____" shown above.

"Dock", in the strict meaning of the term, refers to the structure (pier, wharf, quay, etc.) to which a boat ties up – **true** or **false**?

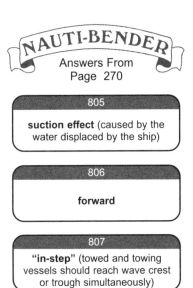

NAUTI-BENDER
Answers From
Page 270

805
suction effect (caused by the water displaced by the ship)

806
forward

807
"in-step" (towed and towing vessels should reach wave crest or trough simultaneously)

The above vessel has laid out two "shot" or _____ feet of chain.

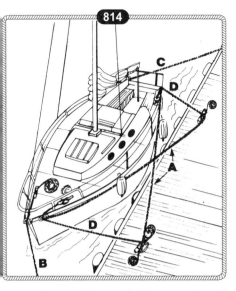

"Breast" lines, "_____" (shown above), hold a boat close to the dock.

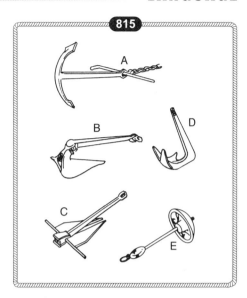

Identify the anchors with the letter shown above: **1. Mushroom 2. Danforth 3. Plough 4. Fisherman 5. Bruce**. Which is typically not carried aboard?

Generally, if your vessel is drifting in calm water, the wind will maneuver your boat until the wind strikes _____.

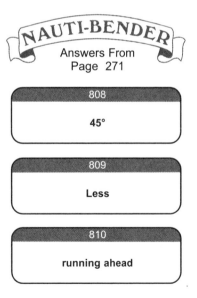

NAUTI-BENDER
Answers From
Page 271

808

45°

809

Less

810

running ahead

"_____ _____ _____" lights have different groups of flashes at regular intervals.

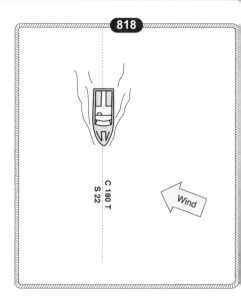

You're proceeding on a 180° true at 22 knots; the apparent wind is from 70° off the port bow at 20 knots. What is true direction/speed of the true wind?

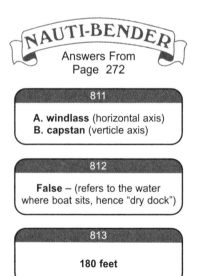

NAUTI-BENDER
Answers From Page 272

811

A. windlass (horizontal axis)
B. capstan (verticle axis)

812

False – (refers to the water where boat sits, hence "dry dock")

813

180 feet

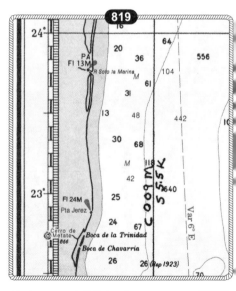

Underway at 5.5 knots on course 009M, Pta Jerez light appears directly off your port beam at 1103 hours. When would you expect to come abeam of R Soto LaMarina Light?

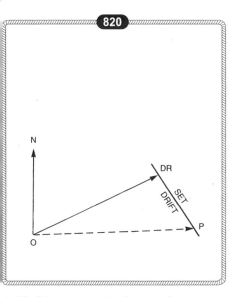

A. "Set" is measured in "_____".
B. "Drift" is measured in "_____".

"_____ _____" lights are illuminated for periods equal to the time of darkness.

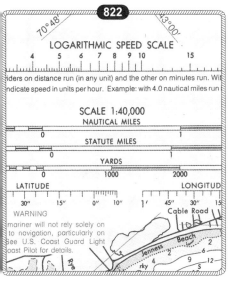

The Rule of Threes: allows for a quick approximation of distance traveled (yards) in three minutes at any multiple of three knots (add two zeroes). How far would you travel in six minutes at nine knots?

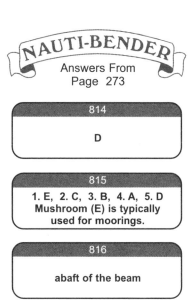

NAUTI-BENDER

Answers From
Page 273

814

D

815

1. E, 2. C, 3. B, 4. A, 5. D
Mushroom (E) is typically
used for moorings.

816

abaft of the beam

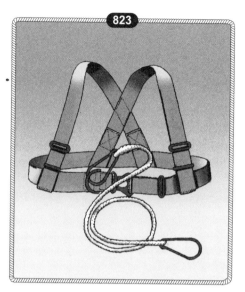

A safety harness should be worn **at any time** when you begin to feel _____ or at night, rough weather, sailing single-handed, and/or when out of sight of other crew.

Most onboard fires/explosions occur shortly after _____.

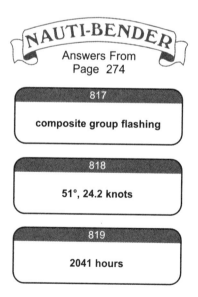

Engine Fire: head boat **into** or **with** the wind; shut down engine and secure fuel supply; then extinguish fire by: **dousing with water**, **Type B** extinguisher or **Type C** extinguisher.

FOAM
FREON (HALON)
CARBON DIOXIDE
DRY CHEMICAL

Which type of fire extinguisher (A) **halon**, (B) **carbon dioxide**, (C) **dry chemical**, or (D) **all of the above** should be checked annually by weight?

The Coast Guard has a rule-of-thumb regarding hypothermia (the 50/50/50 rule): if a person has been in **50°** F water for **50** minutes, he/she has a **50%** _____ _____ _____.

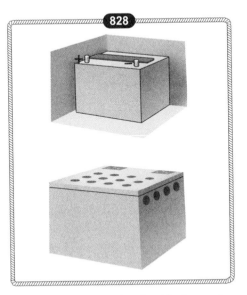

Battery compartments should always be well ventilated to: (A) **avoid carbon dioxide buildup**, (B) **ensure an adequate supply of oxygen for batteries operation**, (C) **avoid accumulation of explosive vapors**.

NAUTI-BENDER
Answers From
Page 275

820
A: degrees
B: knots

821
equal interval or "isophase"

822
1800 yards

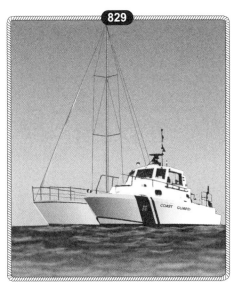

VHF communications – which of the following channels is typically utilized for Coast Guard Communications: **13**, **16**, **22A**, **24**, **27**, **71** or **72**?

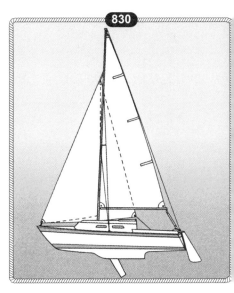

The primary purpose of a sailboat's keel or center board is to prevent the boat from _____ _____ while under sail.

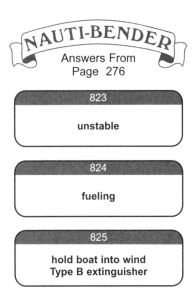

NAUTI-BENDER
Answers From Page 276

823

unstable

824

fueling

825

hold boat into wind
Type B extinguisher

At night, a dim light on the horizon will be seen more quickly by looking: (A) **a little below**, (B) **a little above**, (C) **well below**, or (D) **right at the horizon**.

832

The water-ski hand-signal shown above indicates: _____.

833

Photo courtesy of Tiara Yachts by: Forest Johnson

Rule-of-thumb (tender engine size): to achieve a max speed of 25 knots, divide the boat's weight (loaded) by _____ to determine the required horse power of the engine.

834

When contacting another boat via VHF radio, the transmission should be "Greylag, this is Albacore WS 3976 _____ _____ _____ _____ _____ _____ over.

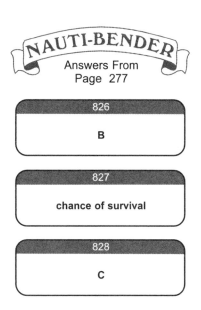

NAUTI-BENDER
Answers From
Page 277

826

B

827

chance of survival

828

C

Sometimes masking tape will lift adjoining areas being painted or varnished. This problem can be avoided by passing the tape across your pants _____ to masking.

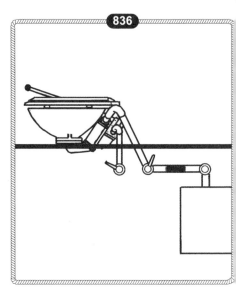

After winter layup your boat's "head" is not working. You determine the discharge line is clogged with waste. Your best approach would be to: flush the line with a mild solution of **sulphuric acid**, **muriatic acid**, or **lye/vinegar**.

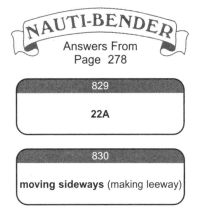

NAUTI-BENDER
Answers From
Page 278

829
22A

830
moving sideways (making leeway)

831
B (a little above the horizon)

Outboard Winterization: the oil in a _____-stroke engine should be changed each season. Dirty oil contains acids that can ruin bearings during long-term inactivity.

Polishing non-skin areas on fiberglass boats is much easier if a _____ _____ rag is utilized.

Smoke from exhaust (diesel engine): _____ _____ smoke is the normal color for proper operation.

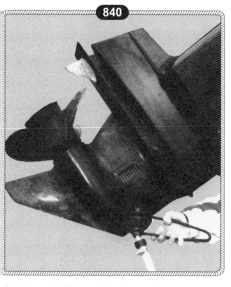

Outboard Winterization: fill fuel tank adding correct amount of stabilizer then **run engine for ten minutes** or **drain fuel system** to prevent gum or varnish formation.

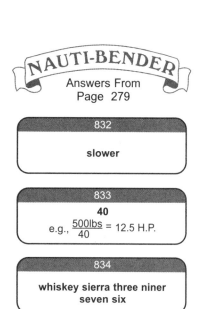

NAUTI-BENDER
Answers From
Page 279

832
slower

833
40
e.g., $\frac{500lbs}{40} = 12.5$ H.P.

834
whiskey sierra three niner seven six

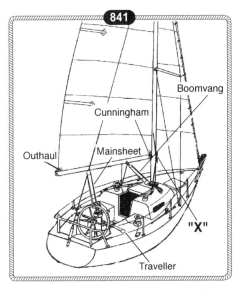

841

Sail Language: "**X**" shown above would be referred to as the "_____", which runs up the mast and is used to raise the sail.

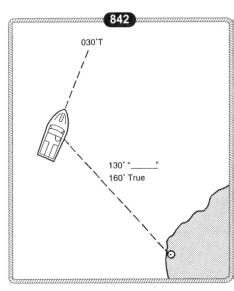

842

030°T

130° "_____"
160° True

"_____ _____" is the direction in relation to the fore- and aft-line of a vessel expressed in degrees.

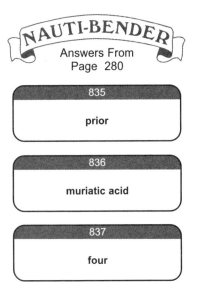

NAUTI-BENDER
Answers From
Page 280

835
prior

836
muriatic acid

837
four

843

When two or more boats are tied side by side at a mooring or dock, it is called "_____".

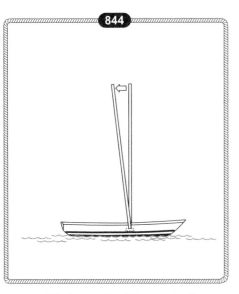

844

"_____" is the angle of the mast, stem, or stern. "_____" is the curvature of the deck as seen from the side.

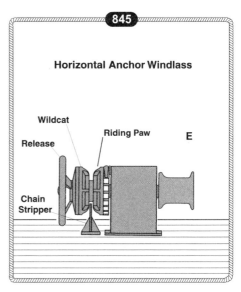

845

Horizontal Anchor Windlass

Wildcat

Riding Paw

E

Release

Chain Stripper

Windlass Nomenclature: "**E**" shown above is referred to as the "_____" and is used to haul in the anchor rode or other lines.

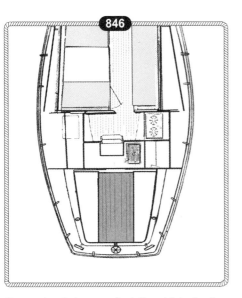

846

Every boat has a "sole", which is the _____ of the cabin or cockpit.

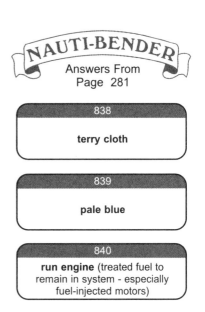

NAUTI-BENDER
Answers From
Page 281

838

terry cloth

839

pale blue

840

run engine (treated fuel to remain in system - especially fuel-injected motors)

In fog, extra care and vigilance should be taken when approaching sea buoys because numerous vessels could be heading for the _____ navigational aid!

A "_____" is a single-masted boat in which the sail area is equally divided between the main sail and more than one "_____ _____".

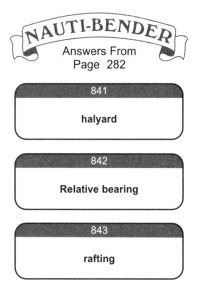

NAUTI-BENDER
Answers From
Page 282

841
halyard

842
Relative bearing

843
rafting

When cruising in a heavy sea you note that your propeller is being lifted clear of the water. One corrective action would be to **increase** or **decrease** speed.

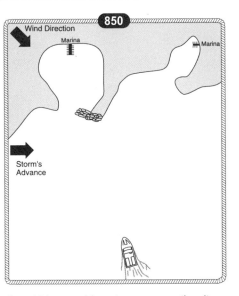

Caught in a sudden storm, one option (typically the last resort), would include riding it out or heaving to in _____ water.

You're sailing on a close-reach when a gust of wind suddenly heels the boat hard over. To reduce the heeling while maintaining speed, you should ease the main and bear more **into** or **away** from the wind.

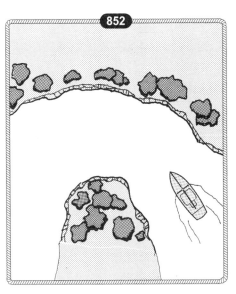

To keep your vessel in the deepest water you should keep close to the _____ bend of a river.

NAUTI-BENDER
Answers From
Page 283

844
Rake **Sheer**

845
gypsy or gypsy head

846
floor or deck

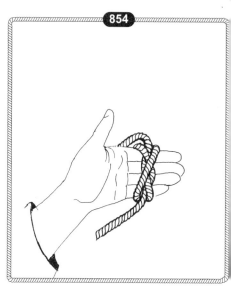

The "_____" (shown above) hitch is easy to cast off or release under pressure without slowing the boat.

The "_____" knot is useful for gripping round objects; however, it is difficult to untie.

Double the life of your dock lines: when they start getting worn, try reversing end-for-end so the chafing point changes. This procedure is sometimes referred to as "_____".

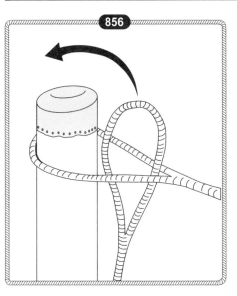

The "_____ _____ _____" method allows either line to be removed without disturbing the other.

"_____ _____", a general term to describe the anchor, rode, fittings, etc., used for anchoring a boat.

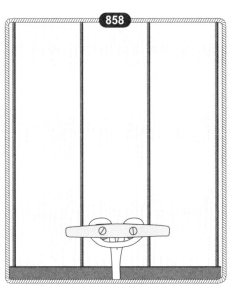

The above depicts the proper method to secure an "eye" to an on-board cleat that will hold well under _____ strain.

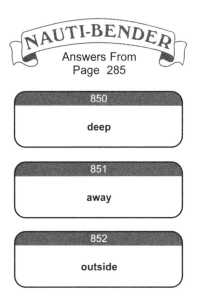

NAUTI-BENDER
Answers From
Page 285

850

deep

851

away

852

outside

859

"Warming up" your engine is accomplished better **idling at dock** or at about **half-speed under load**?

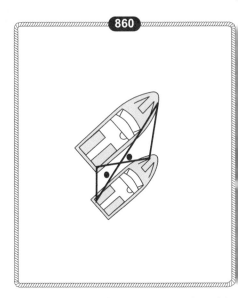

860

If you were planning on towing alongside and you had to maneuver a series of four, sharp right-hand turns, which side of the disabled vessel would you tie-up to?

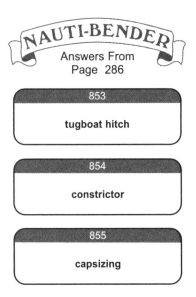

NAUTI-BENDER
Answers From Page 286

853

tugboat hitch

854

constrictor

855

capsizing

861

To estimate your _____ in fog: drop a small ball of paper overboard and note the time it takes to disappear. The navigator can then work out the distance.

862

Typically, the fastest point of sailing is achieved in a "_____ _____" configuration, shown in _____ above.

863

Utilizing two "_____" will help prevent towed dinghies from roaming about, yawing etc.

864

If executed properly, running an inlet (high, following sea) on the back of wave is quite effective; however, running too far _____ may result in broaching or pitchpoling, or too far _____ may result in being pooped.

NAUTI-BENDER
Answers From
Page 287

856
dipping the eye

857
ground tackle

858
no strain

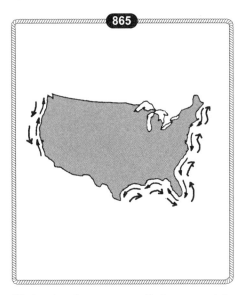

"Returning from seaward", in general is considered to be **clockwise** or **counterclockwise** around the Atlantic, Gulf, and Pacific coasts?

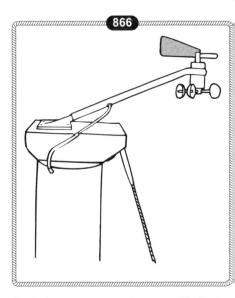

A wind vane on a moving vessel indicates the **true** or **apparent** wind direction.

NAUTI-BENDER

Answers From
Page 288

859

At half speed under load (Long periods of idling are bad for mechanical components.)

860

port side

861

visibility

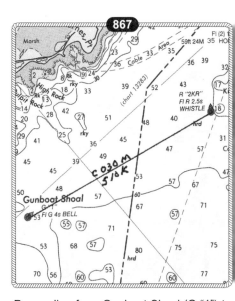

Proceeding from Gunboat Shoal (G "1") to "2KR", a 25-knot wind quickly comes up from 90° relative, affecting your vessel with a 10° "leeway". What course should you now steer.

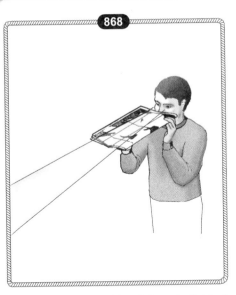

Having difficulty identifying individual islands within a cluster: scan across a folded chart with your eye just above your vessel's _____ toward the islands.

"_____" lights show a flash at intervals with the period of light longer than the period of darkness.

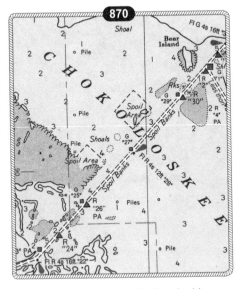

"**PA**" adjacent to a navigational aid on a chart means its _____ _____ _____.

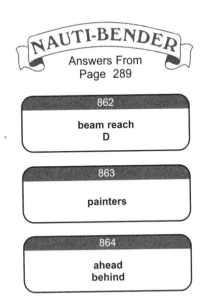

NAUTI-BENDER
Answers From
Page 289

862
beam reach
D

863
painters

864
ahead
behind

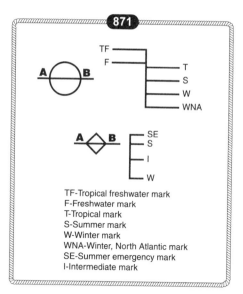

TF-Tropical freshwater mark
F-Freshwater mark
T-Tropical mark
S-Summer mark
W-Winter mark
WNA-Winter, North Atlantic mark
SE-Summer emergency mark
I-Intermediate mark

The "_____", or load line mark, is painted (midships) on both sides of merchant vessels to indicate safe levels of submergence.

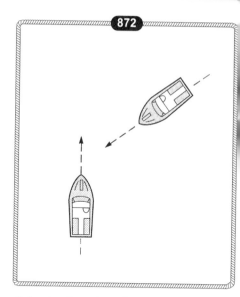

Following the rules of navigation, the "burdened" vessel... has the **right-of-way** (stand-on vessel) or **must give way**?

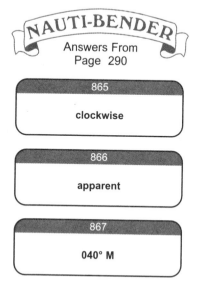

NAUTI-BENDER

Answers From
Page 290

865
clockwise

866
apparent

867
040° M

A line used to tow or tie up a dinghy or tender is called the "_____".

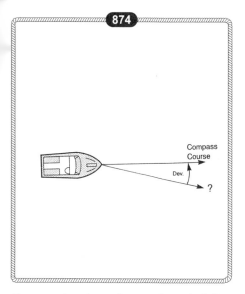

Compass bearings plus or minus deviation amounts will equal "_____" headings.

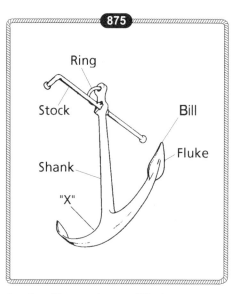

Anchor Nomenclature: "X" shown above would be referred to as the "_____".

What term is used to describe the doing of a task on a boat in a slipshod or sloppy manner?

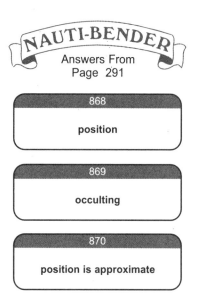

NAUTI-BENDER
Answers From
Page 291

868
position

869
occulting

870
position is approximate

Docking your vessel side-to a pier will be the easiest when the wind and current are _____.

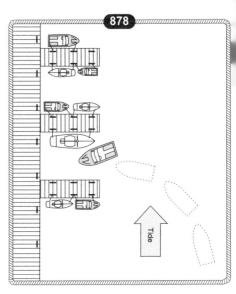

When the stern swings into danger on a turn (single right-handed propeller): what compensating action is required by the skipper?

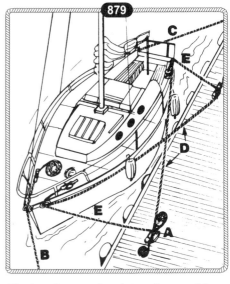

The bow "_____" and stern "_____" lines (shown above) hold the boat fore and aft.

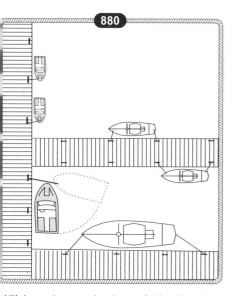

Utilizing a bow spring is useful in situations as shown above with the engine slow _____ with hard _____ rudder.

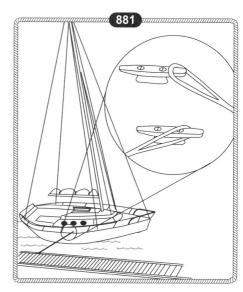

Single handed, spring-line departures are made easier using the cleat quick-release technique (shown above) which will hold well under _____, yet release easily after the maneuver.

When departing, which line should normally be cast off last?

NAUTI-BENDER
Answers From
Page 293

874
magnetic

875
crown

876
lubberly

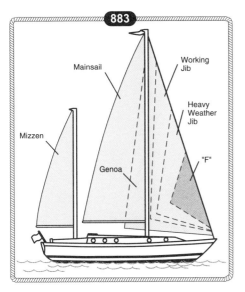

The sail indicated in "**F**" (shown above) is referred to as the "_____ _____".

The "lee" is the direction **toward** or **away** from which the wind is blowing.

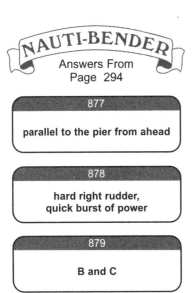

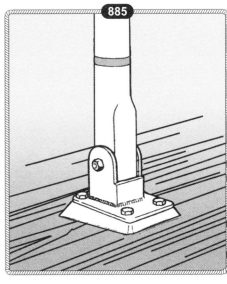

"_____": a fitting, typically made of metal, fixed to a sailing vessel's deck in which the "foot" of a lowering mast is "stepped".

886

A vessel's vertical motion as its bow rises and falls is referred to as "_____".

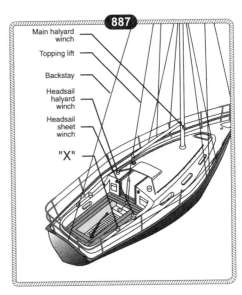

887

Main halyard winch
Topping lift
Backstay
Headsail halyard winch
Headsail sheet winch

"X"

Sail Language: "**X**", shown above, would be referred to as the _____ _____ _____.

888

GREY
Bost

An easily stowed boarding ladder (shown above) which has wooden rungs supported by rope on either side is referred to as a "_____ ladder".

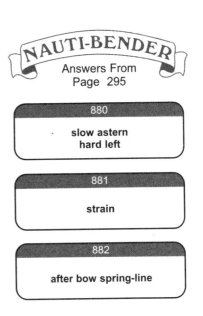

NAUTI-BENDER
Answers From
Page 295

880
**slow astern
hard left**

881
strain

882
after bow spring-line

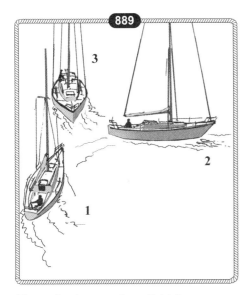

It's easier to execute a tight turn **up-** or **down-wind** (as shown above): **(2)** going ahead the wind will blow the bow around; **(3)** then in reverse the "_____-_____" will kick the stern around.

When towing, always start off gently and gradually build way until you have reached a moderate towing speed – never exceed the disabled boat's "_____ _____".

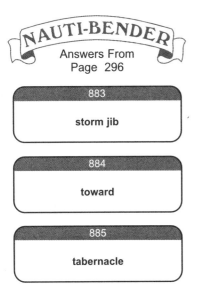

NAUTI-BENDER

Answers From Page 296

883
storm jib

884
toward

885
tabernacle

"_____ _____" spinnakers remain flat under pressure, enabling course runs under "close reach".

892

The quickest way to stop a boat under sail is to: **drop the sails**; **put the engine in reverse**; **steer directly into the wind**; or **throw out the anchor**?

893

A mizzen staysail can be set by a ketch or a yawl on a "_____" or "_____".

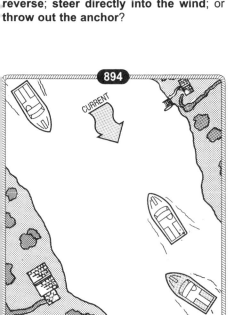

894

When going downstream in a swift current, it sometimes becomes difficult to control the vessel's speed and direction. What corrective measure could the skipper take?

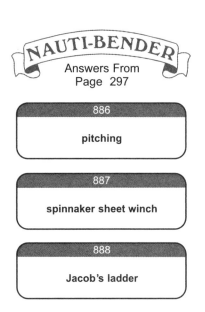

NAUTI-BENDER
Answers From
Page 297

886

pitching

887

spinnaker sheet winch

888

Jacob's ladder

Federal law requires boating accidents involving fatalities, injuries needing more than first aid, or property damage of more than $_____ to be reported to Coast Guard or state authorities.

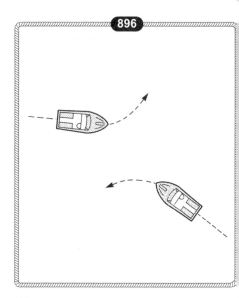

When in doubt between a "crossing" and "head-on" situation, assume a _____ situation.

NAUTI-BENDER
Answers From Page 298

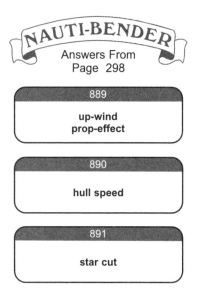

889
up-wind **prop-effect**

890
hull speed

891
star cut

On a river, the **up-** or **down-bound** vessel has the right-of-way?

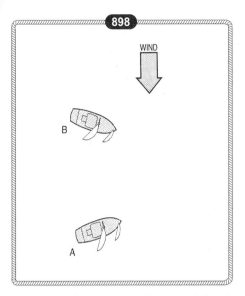

898

WIND

B

A

Which boat (shown above) has the right-of-way or is the "stand-on" vessel?

899

Operating a vessel while intoxicated is a federal offense subject to civil penalty not to exceed $_____ or criminal penalty not to exceed $_____, and/or _____ year(s) imprisonment.

900

How many miles offshore must you be to legally discharge garbage (bottles, cans, food waste etc.) overboard: **3NM**, **6NM**, **12NM**, or **25NM**?

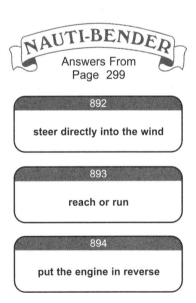

NAUTI-BENDER
Answers From
Page 299

892
steer directly into the wind

893
reach or run

894
put the engine in reverse

You're cruising offshore on a beautiful clear and sunny day, the sea state is calm, but with large swells indicating the presence of a **distant** or **imminent** storm.

Sailors use a scale of 0 to 12 to describe the wind's force, a system developed by the British Rear Admiral Sir Francis _____.

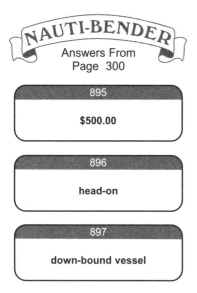

NAUTI-BENDER

Answers From
Page 300

895

$500.00

896

head-on

897

down-bound vessel

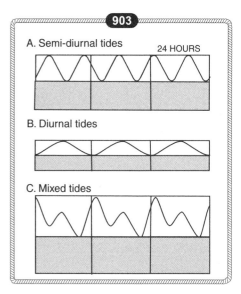

Which of the above **A**, **B**, or **C** illustrates tidal flow normally associated with the tropics?

In different parts of the world, tropical storms (winds 64K plus) are referred to by different names – USA: hurricane; China: _____; India: _____; Australia: _____.

When a high-tide exceeds average height... the following low-tide will be **higher** or **lower** than average?

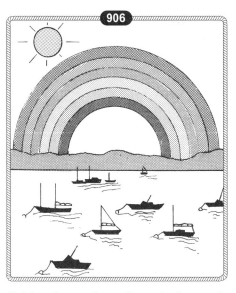

Rainbow in morning, sailors take "_____"; Rainbow at night, sailors "_____".

NAUTI-BENDER
Answers From
Page 301

898
A

899
$1,000.00
$5,000.00
one year

900
12 NM

The best tool to free a propeller fouled with rope is: **a razor-sharp fillet knife**, **a hacksaw**, or **an electrician's side-cutter pliers**.

VHF Communications – which of the following channels should be utilized for contacting the bridge tender: **13**, **16**, **22A**, **24**, **27**, **71** or **72**?

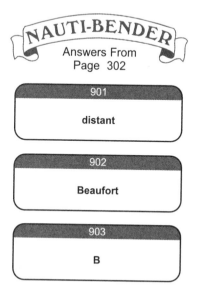

NAUTI-BENDER
Answers From
Page 302

901
distant

902
Beaufort

903
B

In an anchorage (light wind conditions)... why do powerboats and sailboats sometimes point in different directions?

A vessel is said to have been "_____" when a "following" sea overtakes her and breaks over the stern.

When offshore, in conditions that make it almost impossible to maintain headway, it is time to "_____ _____".

After distress call, the radio signal indicating **resume normal radio operation** is "_____ _____".

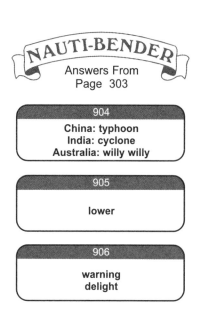

NAUTI-BENDER
Answers From
Page 303

904
China: typhoon
India: cyclone
Australia: willy willy

905
lower

906
warning
delight

305

Answers From
Page 304

907

hacksaw (dull blade)

908

13

909

Tidal flow or current has
more or less effect on
different keel configurations

Answers From
Page 305

910

pooped

911

time to heave to

912

SEELONCE FEENEE

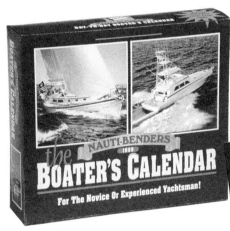